THE HILL

By HOWARD FAST

THE HILL

an original screenplay

by Howard Fast

Doubleday & Company, Inc.
Garden City, New York
1964

THE CAST

AN INTRODUCTION

Mount Morris Park, in Harlem in New York City, is an improbable lump of rock, perhaps half a dozen acres in area and, I would guess, about a hundred feet high. Its southern side makes the northern boundary of 120th Street; it abuts Fifth Avenue, stretches eastward to Madison Avenue and westward half a block from Fifth. Paths gouged out of the native rock or built onto it wind their way up to the summit, and there, on the flat rock of its top, is an iron tower and a flagpole; and as one stands there, all around one, the city and its rooftops. I know of nothing in New York City quite as bizarre, and as unbelievable as Mount Morris Park.

Certainly the physical existence of Mount Morris Park is part of the reason why I wrote *The Hill*; and much of the rest of the reason lies in the accumulating distaste with which I observed the film industry's efforts to tell the story of the life and death of Jesus Christ.

It is said that every serious writer will, in his own time and way, put down his version of the Passion of Christ—not simply because of the compelling dramatic content of this story, but because, regardless of religion, each generation relives the mortal dilemma and agony of the man who dies for all other men. For the same reason, the story demands an approach that is holy in its veracity and truthful in its artistry.

Both of these demands have been ignored by the film industry, and the endless spate of Biblical films that pour out of the dream factories of Hollywood and Rome have no real relationship to the story of the death of a Jewish carpenter two thousand years ago or to the meaning of His Passion. Instead, we are treated to ridiculous posturing in costumes that never encase people, but only stars and extras; we are subjected to the lowest level of Sunday school tedium without love or compassion to soften the boredom; we must endure cowboy-and-Indian, cops-and-robbers plot manufacturing; overdressed boobs labeled Romans and talking in British accents; blundering do-gooders labeled Jews and talking in American accents—and as much sex as will draw audience without damning the so-called "family appeal" of these "bathrobe" monstrosities, as they are known in the trade. But the "family" nature of these offerings is never permitted to dull the great doses of brutality and sheer sadism with which they are concocted.

That they have been and will be endured is due to the fact that, here in America, it is poor politics to attack anything, even blasphemy, if it is wrapped in a container labeled religion. Also, the sheer size and expense of these renderings place an awful burden upon the film reviewers. To expose these films for what they are might well jeopardize the existence of a studio, and thereby endanger the jobs of thousands. Not an enviable position for a reviewer to be placed in.

I wrote *The Hill* as my own protest against the distortion of a profoundly meaningful story. I placed the central movement of the film on Mount Morris Park because this seemed to me to be a modern Hill of Calvary if ever there was one, this crag of rock looming out of a ghetto of the oppressed and the dispossessed, and I took the approach of the Miracle Play of the Middle Ages—that is, I tell the story in the terms, the symbols, and the speech of today, accepting the anachronisms and the non sequiturs, and using them without attempting to explain them.

Just as it would have been impossible to explain to an English peasant of the fourteenth century the philosophy and folkways of Palestinian Jews at the beginning of our era, or the extremely complex nature of their bondage under Rome, so is it equally difficult to explain these facts today. Yet today, as in the fourteenth century, there is a set of parallel symbols that bring us closer to the truth than any scholarly research project might. In the fourteenth century the peasant and townsman accepted these symbols because they were a valid part of his culture. He knew that the people of ancient Judea wore clothes that were different and spoke in another tongue; he also knew that the essential truth was in recognition, and the Miracle Play gave him a means of recognition.

So here, in *The Hill*, I have sought to present the elements of recognition. The word *Negro* never appears in the screenplay; it does not have to, for the play is thought of in terms of the population that lives in the area around the Hill, the heart of the Negro ghetto in Harlem—and so, dealing in symbols of the life there, it would be played by a Negro cast quite naturally.

My blueprint for its construction has been the Gospel according to Mark, and while not dealing with the whole of the Gospel—which I chose because it is the simplest and most dramatically achieved of the four—I have attempted to express the spirit of it. One cannot project or excuse an artistic work by saying that this one or that one delights in it; a work must stand by itself; but so far, none of the clerics in the three great faiths of America who read the manuscript of *The Hill* have been either offended or astonished by it, and a number of them have been most eager to see it in film. Certain laymen, however, have been religiously intimidated—self-intimidated, I must stress—and a good many film financiers have backed away because they fear the very nature of the religious presentation. Others have been unable to accept the manner of its setting, and one of the reasons the film was not produced in the first flush of excitement about its creation was that the financial interests concerned demanded that the final scene on Mount Morris Park be changed or omitted. Here we had a basic unwillingness to accept the challenge and the form of the Miracle Play.

Comparatively few screenplays are written as originals, and even fewer are written entirely upon the speculation of the writer, as was *The Hill*. One reason for this is that the very large sums of money required for the production of a film—even a low-budget film—are controlled by comparatively few sources, and that true independent production is severely limited and very difficult. Another reason lies in custom and precedent. Traditionally, the film in America has based itself upon the novel or the play, and therefore its development as an original and creative form has been severely limited.

While the effort to do *The Hill* as a film was under way, a copy came into the hands of my editors at Doubleday. It was due to their excitement over the material—an excitement shared by other people at Doubleday—that the decision was made to publish the material as a book.

Needless to say, I was delighted at this turn of events. I had not intended *The Hill* as something to be read. I wrote it as a technical thing—a narration in pictures and dialogue, which is what a film is in terms of its form. Yet, re-reading it, I see that it has a certain validity in literary terms, although the terms are rather different and new. A good many screenplays have been published, but not so many as to do away with the novelty of the form. For this reason, I am leaving the form more or less unchanged, so that it may perhaps have some value for those who propose to work in this medium.

In reading, remember that your eyes are the eyes of a camera. As the camera moves, the scene changes. As the camera is your eyes, so, in turn, it will be the eyes of this character or of that one. That is what is meant by *pov*, point of view. The camera will shift its point of view, permitting us to see, first through the eyes of this character, then through the eyes of another. When the camera trucks, it moves on a smooth-wheeled base. I think that the other terms used are self-explanatory.

What follows is not the final shooting script, but still very close to it.

THE HILL

1. EXT. STREET

At the edge of Mount Morris Park, Peter, Cariot, and Andrew as they wait for Joshua. Both men are in their middle thirties. Peter is tall, large of bulk, a fisherman by trade. He wears hip boots, a blue pea jacket against the winter wind, stocking cap. Andrew is a construction worker, metal hat, working clothes. He carries his lunch box. Cariot wears a business suit, shirt and tie.

They stand together, hunched against the cold.

2. EXT. THEIR POV

With their POV, we pick up Joshua coming down the street —a man of medium size, lean, wiry. He wears work trousers, work shoes, and a blue denim shirt. A short canvas coat, sheepskin collar.

He sees Peter and Andrew; his face lights with an engaging smile—a muted smile of greeting.

3. EXT. STREET

The four men, Peter, Cariot, Andrew, and Joshua, stand

together a moment. Peter looks up. Joshua follows his look and nods.

4. EXT. THEIR POV MOUNT MORRIS PARK

The high rock as they see it.

5. EXT. AGAINST MOUNT MORRIS PARK

A *WIDER SHOT* of the four men as they enter the park, with the rock looming in front of them. We see them from some distance as they begin their climb upward. Joshua in front, the others slightly behind him.

6. EXT. IN MOUNT MORRIS PARK. ANOTHER ANGLE

As they climb.

7. EXT. IN MOUNT MORRIS PARK. ANOTHER ANGLE

Picking them up and framing them against background of sky and buildings as they climb.

8. EXT. IN MOUNT MORRIS PARK. ANOTHER PATHWAY

James, John, and Matthew. Three men in their early thirties, working men. James, Matthew, and John are in plain work clothes.
They move toward the top of Mount Morris Park along another pathway.

9. EXT. MOUNT MORRIS PARK

As we pick up people moving toward the top of the rock,

men, women, children, about thirty people, but not all immediately. A gradually converging group.

10. EXT. THE TOP OF THE PARK

As Joshua, Peter, Cariot, and Andrew move up onto the plateau on the top of the park.

11. EXT. THE TOP OF THE PARK. ANOTHER ANGLE

James, John, and Matthew join Peter and Andrew. Joshua has separated himself from them. Apparently lost in thought, he moves toward the upthrust of rock at the flagpole. Others are coming onto the top.

12. EXT. THE TOP. JOSHUA

CLOSE-UP on Joshua as he stands by the flagpole, his expression turned inward upon himself. Bent slightly, he raises his head now and surveys the scene. We pick up his *POV*.

13. EXT. THE TOP. JOSHUA'S POV

We sweep the horizon, the rooftops, the distant canyon of Park Avenue, the abutments of the Triboro Bridge—and then the little crowd gathering on the top.

14. EXT. THE TOP. CLOSE ON DISCIPLES

The faces of the six men, their eyes fixed on Joshua.

15. EXT. THE TOP. PANNING

On other faces of people on the top, Jairus, his daughter, a child of ten or so, Sarah, Joshua's cousin, two of the judges, Philip and Thomas among them.

16. EXT. THE TOP. SKY AND BUILDINGS

Against this, Joshua's voice:

JOSHUA

My brother came to me, and he was filled with hate,
like a cup is filled with water. He was sick, and I
cured him. It is no miracle, but simple love that
cures hate and fear.

ON JOSHUA NOW, CLOSE

Enough love and enough faith, and the world will
rise up like a shining tower. So simple, yet it's the
hardest thing in the whole world—just the hardest
thing in the whole world.

17. EXT. THE TOP. PANNING ON THE FACES

The crowd has increased, and we see the reaction on their
faces as Joshua speaks.

JOSHUA

(cont'd)
Why do you doubt me? You come to me and plead
with me, Joshua do this, Joshua do that, Joshua,
make it right—but only you can make it right. You
can look at your hands, because your strong hands
built the whole world. Do you ever look into your
heart?

ON JOSHUA

You're the salt of the earth, but when the salt becomes flat and tasteless—how do you salt it then?
With what? You got a right arm with the kick of a
trip hammer, but not enough strength to love your

brother. What does God ask of you? I tell you it's
all in one simple, plain thing—love your brother as
yourself—

18. EXT. THE TOP. JOSHUA

He stands alone by the flagpole as the crowd begins to melt
away. Four of his disciples stand waiting for him, Peter,
Andrew, Cariot, and James. The CAMERA draws back, so
that we have a whole view of the top emptying. Then CLOSE
on Joshua, who is turned inward, almost in grief, as if ob-
sessed by a sense of his own futility.

19. EXT. MOUNT MORRIS. LONG SHOT

Of Joshua and the four disciples as they come down from
the rock.

20. EXT. TEMPLE. JUDGE (*priest 1*)

INTERCUT of the front of the TEMPLE. FIRST PRIEST
stands there, watching Joshua in distance. The Priest is an
old man. Ministerial garb. We return to 19 with priest's
POV.

INTERCUT 19.

21. EXT. STREET. JOEY. FRANKIE. BUTTONS

Three boys, as old as eighteen and less than twenty, nervous, neurotic, twisted, and filled with hate and anxiety. Their
boastfulness is a compensation for inadequacy, their hostility
the other side of their fear. They are hooked on dope and
driven by demons. They are petty thieves, cheap crooks, hit-
and-run muggers; and deeply pathetic in that what is human
in them is still visible.

Out of a necessity to believe in something, they believe in
Joshua. He is the only one they know who has never reviled
them, never blamed them, never accused them, never re-
jected them. They sense that he is better, perhaps, than
others, and they bring him the only offerings they have, their
warped dreams and their witless schemes. He takes the place
of father, mother, and confessor.

They fall in with him as he walks up the street, his disciples a little behind him. Whatever they say, there is no
shred of disrespect for Joshua.

JOEY

Joshua!

FRANKIE

We got to talk, man.

BUTTONS

We're swinging. We got it big, this time, Joshua—
big, man, big!

FRANKIE

You been up on the hill, Joshua?

JOSHUA

(*still turned inward*)
I been up on the hill.

FRANKIE

Man, you shoulda told us. That's preaching. That's
cool preaching up on that hill.

JOEY

We got to talk to you, Joshua.

JOSHUA

All right. Talk to me.

BUTTONS

Not here, Joshua. Can we come to the shop? About an hour?

JOSHUA

All right. In an hour.

INTERCUT PETER'S face during the last of this. Hard, grave.

The three boys take off.

22. EXT. STREET. PETER AND JOSHUA. TWO SHOT TRUCKING

PETER

So help me, Joshua, I fail to comprehend you.

JOSHUA

I talk plainly, Peter.

PETER

You know what I mean.

JOSHUA

(*almost angrily*)
I wish I didn't know what you mean.

PETER

They're no good, those kids—no good! Rotten little
punks. They'd kill their mothers for kicks.

JOSHUA

All right, what do we do—kill them?

PETER

I say there are decent people need you.

JOSHUA

(*angrily*)
I say no! The sick need me! What am I, a physician
to the healthy? Shall I make the strong stronger?
Is there no place in the world for the weak, the lost,
the forgotten? Do you know why those boys come to
me?

He turns on Peter almost fiercely and *TRUCKING* stops.
The camera opens into a wider shot to include Cariot, Andrew, and James.

FULL NOW

Peter shakes his head.

JOSHUA

Why? Why do they come to me? What are you,
fisherman? Did I ever say to you that I would make
you a fisher for men?
     (*He turns on Andrew.*)
And you—builder! Did we never speak of another
structure, inside a man?
     (*gentle again*)

All right. All right. The boys come to me because
whatever they bring me, I accept it with love. Don't
ask me to send them away. Don't ever ask me that.

23. EXT. STREET

Under the last four lines of 22, the setup turns into motion,
and the five men move away from us. We hear their words as
they pass away from us down the street.

24. EXT. JOSHUA'S SHOP

The exterior of a cabinetmaking shop on a side street in
Harlem. On the dusty windows, the words: *CABINET-
WORK FURNITURE REPAIRS FINE JOINING.*
We see the shop first in a full shot that commands most
of the street. Then CLOSER as Joshua goes to the door and
enters.

25. INT. THE SHOP

REVERSE OF 24, as Joshua enters, and then the shop.
An old-fashioned carpentry shop. A counter that runs halfway across the front, and behind the counter two work-
benches equipped with vises. Tools on the walls, a rack of
wood, pieces of broken furniture, parts of furniture, mill
pieces.
As Joshua enters, his father, *JOSEPH*, is at work at one of
the benches, planing a piece of wood grasped in a vise.
Joseph is old, gnarled, bent with work, his vision narrowed
by labor without joy. He greets his son gloomily.

JOSEPH

Where were you?

JOSHUA

*(taking off his coat, hanging it on a peg, and then
putting on a carpenter's apron)*
On the hill, Father.
(His voice is kind, even, and controlled.)

JOSEPH

The hill! The hill! How much more of that?

JOSHUA

As much as I must, Father.

JOSEPH

You must! What? Who tells you that you must go
up on a hill and preach like a damn fool?

JOSHUA

(setting wood in the vise and beginning to work)
I do what I must do.

JOSEPH

A man works and works—he expects something
from his son. Something. I sweated blood to raise
you and give you something a little better than I
got. And you preach. You preach. You practice
magic—

JOSHUA

(tiredly)
Not magic, Father.

JOSEPH

Miracles. Magic. Up there on that hill, day and night. For what? What does it lead to? What comes of it?

The door of the shop opens. *MRS. MARAT* enters. Mrs. Marat is a middle-aged woman, plainly dressed. She carries a small chair, one leg broken off. Joshua comes around the counter, takes the chair from her, and places it on the counter.

JOSHUA

Hello. How are the children, Mrs. Marat?

MRS. MARAT

All right, I suppose. You talk about the children, Joshua—all I say is you got to expect nothing. Give everything; God help you, you expect anything in return.

JOSHUA

Still, it's one kind of love, Mrs. Marat. Maybe the best kind.

MRS. MARAT

What kind?

JOSHUA

To give—and expect nothing in return. But it's not easy either, is it? Let me look at this—

He handles and examines the chair. Meanwhile and during the above dialogue, Joseph goes on working.

JOSHUA

(*cont'd*)

It's old, Mrs. Marat, but the wood is firm and rich.
It's worth fixing. I'll join the leg properly this time.

MRS. MARAT

How much, Joshua?

JOSHUA

I think—two dollars.

Joseph looks up at him, but whatever he intends to say is
cut off by the entrance from outside of Joey, Frankie, and
Buttons. They stand at the side of the door, waiting.
Joshua walks to the door with Mrs. Marat.

JOSHUA

Try not to fret over the kids. Trust them—don't
turn away from them.

MRS. MARAT

It's hard, Joshua.

JOSHUA

Sure it's hard. It's always hard. I'll have the chair in
a few days.

The door closes behind Mrs. Marat. Joseph goes on work-
ing grimly, ignoring the three boys. They gather around
Joshua at the counter, talking softly but not so softly that
Joseph can't hear them.

FRANKIE

This is big, Joshua. No two-bit mugging in the park
—no purse snatching. That's for punks.

BUTTONS

The big time, Joshua. We're going to knock over a
bank.

JOEY

One big, clean job—we got it made.

Joshua stares at them, unbelieving.

BUTTONS

It ain't new, Joshua. We been talking a bank job for
months. Man, we're swinging with it now.

FRANKIE

Plain and simple and clean, Joshua. Joey watches
at the door. I go in with Buttons. We got a paper
bag, see? That's the big routine now. We got this
bag and I shove it through the window and tell the
twist to put money in it. Buttons covers. Put ten
grand in the bag, cookie. Just like that.

JOEY

Tomorrow, Joshua. How about that? What do you
say?

JOSHUA

(*without heat, smiling slightly*)
What do I say? I just say it's the most harebrained

scheme I ever heard. It's senseless. You couldn't knock over a newsstand with a scheme like that.

FRANKIE

Why, Joshua? Why?

JOSHUA

Maybe twenty reasons. Banks have armed guards. Alarm buttons on the floor. Automatic cameras.

FRANKIE

We move quick.

JOSHUA

How quick? Quicker than light? And suppose you got out? How far would you get? Give it up, because it won't work.

BUTTONS

Oh, man, you don't mean that.

JOSHUA

I mean it.

FRANKIE

We can't give it up. This is too big, Joshua.

JOSHUA

I'll buy that. It's too big.

BUTTONS

It can't work?

JOSHUA

That's what I said. Not in a thousand years.

The three of them stare at Joshua. He goes to his work-bench and begins to work again.

JOSEPH

(*pausing in his work to look at the three boys*)
Thieves. Crooks. Rotten bums—get out of here!

JOEY

Easy, Pops—easy.

The outside door bursts open, and *JAIRUS* enters. Panting, he rushes over to the counter. He is a man of about forty, rather short, and normally of a gentle manner. But now he is beside himself with grief, desperate in his supplication.

JAIRUS

Joshua! Joshua, for God's sake, help me!

JOSHUA

What is it, Jairus? What happened?

JAIRUS

(*half sobbing*)
My daughter—she's dead.

The three boys freeze into motionless silence; death still reaches them and touches them. Joseph puts down his tools and turns to face Jairus. Joshua speaks with deep sympathy.

JOSHUA

I'm sorry. Poor child.
  (*He comes around the counter and puts an arm
  around Jairus.*)
I know your grief—I know—

JAIRUS

  (*pulling away*)
Help me, Joshua—help me.

JOSHUA

As much as I can. Yes—

JAIRUS

  (*with desperate intensity*)
Raise her, Joshua. Please raise her. Give her back to
me. She's all we have—

JOSHUA

If the child's dead, Jairus, I can only pray for her
soul and try to comfort you.

JAIRUS

You work miracles, Joshua. Raise her from the dead.

JOSHUA

  (*sharply*)
Jairus! What kind of talk is that? Only God can raise
the dead.

JAIRUS

(*utterly bereft in his pleading*)
Joshua—Joshua, don't be angry with me—

JOSHUA

(*shaking his head sadly*)
I'm not angry, Jairus—

JAIRUS

Help me. Our only child, Joshua. Help me—please
help me.

JOSHUA

I'll help you, Jairus. Come, we'll go to her.

He takes down his coat, and then opens the door for
Jairus. They exit. The three boys still remain motionless.
Joseph stares after Joshua.

JOSEPH

(*suddenly, bitterly*)
You three—get out! Get out!

The boys come to life. They stand for a moment, grinning
at Joseph. Their tension disappears. They slouch.

FRANKIE

OK, Popsie—OK. Take it easy.

They exit. From the apartment back of the shop, MARY,
Joseph's wife, enters. She is a woman in her fifties, work-
worn, soft of speech, and gentle in manner.

MARY

I thought I heard Jairus.

JOSEPH

He was here.

MARY

His voice was full of grief.

JOSEPH

(*returning to work at the bench*)
He got his grief. His daughter's dead.

MARY

Oh, God help him, poor man—poor man—

26.   EXT. FRONT OF SHOP

The three boys on the street.

FRANKIE

You dig that? Man come in—Joshua, raise the dead.
How about that?

BUTTONS

Crazy, man—crazy.

JOEY

He can do it. I tell you, Joshua can do it.

FRANKIE

Man, you're flying. You're out of your mind. No one can't raise the dead.

JOEY

Joshua can do any damn thing in the world, he just puts his mind to it.

FRANKIE

You crazy? What you think Joshua is—some kind of god?

JOEY

He different. I tell you that. Different. Ain't no one else like him—no one.

BUTTONS

(*dreamily, motioning with his hands*)
Raise the dead. Cool, man—cool.

27. EXT. STREET

As Joshua and Jairus turn a corner into a side street, a two shot.

28. EXT. SIDE STREET. JOSHUA'S POV

After turning, a cut from two shot to Joshua's POV down the street. A shabby, rundown street of tenements and brownstones. Halfway down the street an ambulance is backed at an angle to the curb. A crowd of curious people around it, men, women, and kids.

INTERCUT on Joshua and Jairus.

INTERCUT high angle full shot, possibly rooftop, as Joshua and Jairus approach the crowd.

29. EXT. STREET. CROWD

As Joshua and Jairus push through the crowd into the tenement.

INTERCUT close-up on Jairus.

INTERCUT another angle on Joshua and Jairus.

30. INT. TENEMENT HALLWAY AND DOOR. REVERSE OF 29

As Joshua and Jairus come through the door and into the hallway.

31. INT. STAIRWELL OF TENEMENT

ANGLE SHOT as Joshua and Jairus climb the stairs. A single flight of stairs. The *CAMERA* should be directed downward from above. They enter the flat.

32. INT. JAIRUS'S APARTMENT. THE KITCHEN

The main entrance to the apartment is through the kitchen, as is most often the case with the old flats. As Jairus and Joshua enter, Jairus dragging Joshua through a crowd of people.

33. INT. JAIRUS'S APARTMENT. PARLOR

As Joshua and Jairus pass through. Women are here, neighbors. They are crying. They dab at their faces with their aprons. Here, also, the ambulance driver with portable oxygen equipment.

34. INT. JAIRUS'S APARTMENT. BEDROOM

A small room, crowded, for there is hardly more than enough room for the old brass bed and the few pieces of furniture. Mrs. Jairus stands sobbing, a neighbor attempting to comfort her. The CHILD (*JAIRUS'S DAUGHTER*) lies on the bed, and as Joshua and Jairus enter the INTERN is drawing the sheet over the child's face.

Then the Intern turns to Joshua and Jairus.

> INTERN

I'm sorry. She's dead. We were too late. You should have called us earlier.

As Joshua begins to pass him to the bed.

> INTERN

(*cont'd*)
Who are you?

> JOSHUA

My name's Joshua.

> INTERN

I heard of you. The miracle worker. Well, I told you—the child's dead.

> JOSHUA

(*bending over the bed and drawing back the sheet to reveal a lovely little girl. She lies with her eyes closed, motionless.*)
I don't think so—

INTERN

(*angrily*)
What the devil do you mean?

Jairus stiffens with attention. Mrs. Jairus stops crying and stares at Joshua. The people in the next room crowd the doorway.

JOSHUA

(*touching the child's cheek gently*)
She isn't dead. She sleeps.
(*He speaks slowly, thoughtfully, turned inward.*)

INTERN

You fool—they'll only suffer more! The child's dead. Your miracles can't help her.

JOSHUA

(*almost to himself, as he bends over the child*)
This child isn't dead. She sleeps. I told you that. She sleeps.

He bends over the child, touching her cheeks lightly, and then he kisses her tenderly on the brow. When he straightens up and stands away, he appears suddenly exhausted.

Then, in the frozen moment of silence, the child opens her eyes—and slowly raises herself on one elbow. Sobbing, Mrs. Jairus drops on her knees by the bed, to take the child in her arms.

CLOSE on Jairus, who stands still, the tears running down his face.

CLOSE on the Intern, mouth open, dumfounded.

CLOSE on Joshua, his face curiously sad.

35. INT. BIG ABBEY'S OFFICE

BIG ABBEY is a hard, heavy-set man, the local gang leader, the boss of the numbers racket and prostitution, and saloonkeeper in terms of the local nightclub. He is expensively overdressed, diamond stickpin on his hand-painted silk tie, diamond rings, and white carnation in his lapel.

He sits behind a mahogany desk in his office—the office itself an attempt at dignity and taste that misses widely.

Facing him, the three boys, Frankie, Joey, and Buttons.

> BIG ABBEY
>
> I call a spade a spade. I call a punk a punk.

> FRANKIE
>
> What do we got to do to prove we can handle a job, Big Abbey?

> BIG ABBEY
>
> Grow up.

> JOEY
>
> We don't have to take this crud from nobody.

> BIG ABBEY
>
> The door's right there.

> FRANKIE
>
> Wait a minute, Big Abbey. Just tell me—what you got against us? You heard the job.

> BIG ABBEY
>
> You're hopheads. I don't trust junkies.

FRANKIE

Give us a chance.

BIG ABBEY

(*grinning suddenly*)
OK. I like you, Frankie. I don't give two cents for
these punks, but I like you.
(*He reaches into his desk drawer.*)
Here's the gun.
(*He pushes a Colt revolver across the desk.*)
Just remember—this is no cheap mugging or purse
snatching. A bank job is the big time. We'll have the
car for you in the morning.

BUTTONS

And what's your cut, Big Abbey?

BIG ABBEY

Half. Right down the line—fifty per cent.

PAN on the boys as we cut out of this.

36. EXT. STREET

LONG shot of Joshua as he walks down the street. A sense
of aloneness, long shadows, last sunlight.

37. EXT. FRONT OF JOSHUA'S SHOP

The three boys in front of the shop.

INTERCUT long shot of Joshua approaching downstreet.
Twilight.
The three boys again. *THREE SHOT.*

FRANKIE

Don't tell him about the gun.

BUTTONS

Man, you can tell Joshua anything.

FRANKIE

I say, don't tell him about the gun.

JOEY

Easy, man. You're shook. You got nerve ends show-
ing.

INTERCUT Joshua near them.
Frankie, Joey, Buttons, and Joshua. Four shot.

FRANKIE

Hey, Joshua.

JOEY

We been waiting for you.

FRANKIE

We got it cool, man, cool. We got a heap for the
getaway. It's going to work.

Joshua stares at them without replying. His face is full of
grief.

FRANKIE

You got misery? What's wrong, Joshua?

JOSHUA

Don't do it. It's no good.
(*not accusatory, but a soft statement of fact*)

FRANKIE

Man, it's going to work.

JOSHUA

It won't work. It's hard enough to live—just to live
and earn your daily bread. Why do you make it
harder?

JOEY

You got blues, man. You got such misery. You got
to swing with what we try to do.

FRANKIE

We don't make it harder, Joshua. We going to make
it summertime all year long. We going to be loaded.
Cool and crazy and loaded.

Joshua shakes his head and turns into the shop.

CLOSE on the three boys as they stare after him.

38. INT. THE SHOP. REVERSE OF PREVIOUS. 37

CLOSE on Joshua as he enters, closing the door behind him.

CLOSE on Joseph as he turns toward his son. He is at his
workbench.

WIDE as Joshua walks across the shop and behind the
counter.

JOSEPH

What happened?

Joshua shakes his head, takes off his coat, puts on his work apron.

JOSEPH

(cont'd)
For me, not even a plain answer. For those hoodlums outside, everything.

JOSHUA

I'm sorry.

JOSEPH

I tell you this—you have any sense, you'll call the police. Turn them in!

JOSHUA

Yes—turn them in. Give life to this one, death to another! I am no judge! I am no god! I'm a man and the son of man! Don't ask me to sit in judgment!

39. INT. THE APARTMENT BEHIND THE SHOP. DINING ROOM

Joseph, Joshua, Mary, and Sarah, Joseph's niece, live in a small apartment behind the shop. For our purposes, two rooms of this apartment are used, the kitchen and the dining room. From the back of the shop, one enters the dining room, about ten by fifteen feet, a long, oilcloth-covered table in the center, a long bench on each side of the table, a chair at each end. In one corner, an old-fashioned crystal closet. On the side, a narrow buffet.

The dining room connects with the kitchen.

At the table, Joshua and his father. Joseph is finishing a bowl of soup. Joshua's soup is in front of him, untasted. Joseph sits at the end of the table, Joshua at one side on the bench.

Mary enters from the kitchen.

MARY

Joshua—you haven't touched the soup. Eat a little.

JOSHUA

(*smiling at her*)
I'm not very hungry, Mother.

MARY

It's good soup.

JOSHUA

I know, Mother.

JOSEPH

(*as he finishes his soup*)
A clear conscience would improve the appetite.

MARY

Please—no arguments, no fights at supper. Please.

Mary exits to kitchen.

40. INT. THE KITCHEN

REVERSE of last shot as Mary enters the kitchen.

The kitchen is small, old-fashioned. An ancient refrigerator, coil on top. Early gas stove. Small worktable.

Old iron sink. At the worktable, *SARAH* mashes potatoes. She is in her twenties, slim, attractive, plainly dressed—essentially a gentle person who adores Joshua.

Mary empties a pot of stew into a bowl, to bring it to the table.

> MARY
>
> They're squabbling again. Biting, clawing at each other. I can't stand it. I can't—

> SARAH
>
> Why can't he leave Joshua alone?

> MARY
>
> I don't know. I just don't know. Put the potatoes on a plate.

> SARAH
>
> Wherever Joshua goes, they love him. They crowd around him, just to touch his clothes. In freezing weather, they go up on the hill to hear him preach.

> MARY
>
> I know.

> SARAH
>
> Only here—only here it's different.

MARY

I know. Bring the potatoes in.

SARAH

I heard Joshua say once, almost to himself, a
prophet is not without honor, except in his own
home.

MARY

All right, Sarah, all right. That's enough. Let's have
one dinner in peace.

She exits with the stew. Sarah stands a moment, then puts
the potatoes on a plate and exits.

41. INT. DINING ROOM

Mary is dishing out the stew as Sarah enters from kitchen
with the potatoes. She catches Joshua's eye, and he smiles at
her. She returns the smile.

Mary and Sarah sit down. The family begins to eat in
silence. Joshua has taken a few bites when there is a hammering on the outside door of the shop.

MARY

Who can that be at this hour?

JOSEPH

Miracles for sale. Customers for magic not for
carpentry. And when he gets a customer, it's two
dollars for five dollars of work—

Joshua leaves the table and exits as the hammering on the
outside door continues.

42. INT. THE SHOP

As Joshua comes out of the dining room, and through the shop to answer the door.

Big Abbey is at the door, wearing a greatcoat with a fur collar and a black Homburg. He stamps in, blowing away the cold, and Joshua closes the door behind him.

From *JOSHUA'S POV*, Big Abbey and the door to the dining room behind him. Mary and Sarah are in the doorway, holding aside the curtain that divides it from the shop. Joseph behind them.

BIG ABBEY

Are you the miracle worker? You don't look like much of a miracle worker to me. You don't look like much of anything.

JOSHUA

Big Abbey. Good evening to you.

BIG ABBEY

You know me.

JOSHUA

I know you, yes.

BIG ABBEY

Joshua—Joshua, the carpenter?

JOSHUA

My name's Joshua, yes.

BIG ABBEY

They tell me you heal the sick.

JOSHUA

Go to a physician for that, Big Abbey.

BIG ABBEY

For what? For madness? They say when the soul is sick, you can heal it.

JOSHUA

And you believe in a soul, Big Abbey?

BIG ABBEY

You know what I believe in—
    (*He clenches his fist.*)
This.

JOSHUA

Then use it, Big Abbey. Why do you come to me?

BIG ABBEY

Because I'm a sucker. Because I'm carrying the torch for a dame who's sick—
    (*He taps his head.*)
here—she's sick here. Depression, they call it. She goes dead on me. She's alive but she's dead. For days. I never knew a dame like this, never. But she's sick. She wants you, and I said I'd bring you. That's it. You want money—
    (*He takes out a roll of bills.*)

How much? What do these creeps you deal with
pay you? How much?

JOSHUA

Who is she, this woman you love?

BIG ABBEY

She's a dancer at my club. Her name's Salome.
How much?

JOSHUA

I don't take money for what I do.

BIG ABBEY

When I buy, I pay for it.

JOSHUA

Then go to a physician and pay him.

Big Abbey starts toward the door in anger. His hand on the
knob, he hesitates. Then he turns back to Joshua.

BIG ABBEY

All right. Will you come?

JOSHUA

If I'm needed—yes, I'll come.

He goes to the peg where his coat hangs, takes it down,
puts it on—all the while Big Abbey watching him dubiously
and contemptuously. He opens the door for Big Abbey.

CLOSE THREE SHOT across them to door to apartment.
Mary, Sarah, and Joseph have come into the shop. They stand
there, silently, as Big Abbey exits after Joshua.

43. EXT. FRONT OF SHOP. REVERSE OF 42.
NIGHT

As Joshua and Big Abbey come out of the shop. In front of the shop, a big Cadillac waits, a long, sleek, black limousine. Big Abbey's driver stands next to it, not in uniform, just a hard, tough hoodlum.

He opens the back door for them. Joshua gets in. Big Abbey follows him. The driver closes the door and goes around to the front.

44. EXT. THE STREET. NIGHT

As the car pulls away.

45. EXT. THE NIGHTCLUB

The brightly lit front of the nightclub that is Big Abbey's headquarters as the black limousine pulls up. A uniformed doorman. Richly dressed men and women entering.

46. EXT. ON THE CAR. ANOTHER ANGLE

As the driver comes around to open the door of the car, and Big Abbey and Joshua get out.

FULL SHOT as they cross to enter the *NIGHTCLUB*.

47. INT. THE LOBBY OF THE NIGHTCLUB

As Joshua and Big Abbey enter. Big Abbey is greeted by the headwaiter, the hat-check girl, etc.

Hello, Boss.

Boss.

Hi, Boss.

The hat-check girl takes Big Abbey's hat and coat. She looks at Joshua, who stands at the entrance to the main room.

Big Abbey follows her glance. Then he shakes his head—as to indicate, "Let him wear his coat," and walks over and then leads Joshua into the main room.

48. INT. NIGHTCLUB. THE MAIN ROOM

Big Abbey leads Joshua past the bar. Heads turn to look at him, so out of place here with his canvas work coat, but any comments are halted by the obviously protective presence of Big Abbey.

WIDE SHOT past them into the main room. We see them as they walk into a tightly packed, dimmed room, small tables, people sitting shoulder to shoulder, a dance floor, and behind it a hot jazz combination.

ANOTHER ANGLE as a waiter leads them to the table that is reserved for Big Abbey. This table is on the edge of the dance floor, at the front.

CLOSE as they sit down.

> BIG ABBEY

What do you drink, miracle man? It's on the house.

Joshua shakes his head.

> BIG ABBEY

(*cont'd*)
Sorry. I figured you for a side-show man, not a holy
Joe.

Joshua doesn't seem to hear him. He stares slowly around him at the unfamiliar scene, the posh nightclub, the well-dressed men, the good-looking, heavily-painted women, the jazz combination—and is apparently unperturbed by the fact that so many of them are regarding him curiously.

Then the combination begins, and the trumpet player stands and takes off, whipping the melody up to a wild pitch. The music is modern jazz, pulsating with heat and emotion.

CLOSE on the combination.

CLOSE for reaction on Joshua, on Big Abbey.

FULL SHOT tables, dance floor, and band.

CLOSE on door through which entertainers appear, as *SALOME* appears.

A full-fleshed, strong, and sensuous woman, Salome begins her dance—an exotic and suggestive dance, sexual and almost frenzied, part striptease—part primitive.

She wears very little, her breasts half covered and not much more than a G-string around her thighs. Swaying, gliding, she moves out on the floor.

CLOSE on Salome as she dances.

CLOSE-UP on Big Abbey for reaction.

CLOSE-UP on customers at the tables.

CLOSE-UP on Joshua as he watches her.

ANOTHER ANGLE on Salome in full.

CLOSE-UP on Salome's face as she moves toward Big Abbey's table, and then,

SALOME'S POV to Joshua's face, *CLOSE-UP*

QUICK CUTS back and forth of the two faces, the music rising to a piercing scream behind this, and *QUICK CUTS* to band.

Salome stops. She freezes where she is, staring at Joshua. The music behind her continues, frenzied and high-pitched. Then she whirls and dashes across the floor, back into the entrance from which she had entered, and she exits.

49. INT. NIGHTCLUB. CLOSE ON JOSHUA AND BIG ABBEY

BIG ABBEY

Now what the hell got into her? Now what in hell
made her do that? I told you, miracle man—I told
you she's sick, sick inside.

No answer from Joshua. He simply sits there, watching Big
Abbey.

CLOSE-UP on Joshua's face.

50. INT. HALLWAY BACK OF NIGHTCLUB

As Big Abbey pushes his way through dancers, stagehands,
and musicians. One of his hoodlums follows him, and then
Joshua. They come to the door to Salome's dressing room.
Big Abbey opens the door, the gesture saying in effect that
this is his right.

They enter, Big Abbey, the hoodlum, and Joshua.

51. INTERIOR. THE DRESSING ROOM

WIDE AND ACROSS the crowded dressing room as the
three men enter.

The dressing room is small, about seven by nine feet, a
table for makeup, mirror, lights framing mirror, screen for
changes, rack for clothes, and a chaise. Also, two chairs.

Already in the dressing room as the three men enter,
Salome, her dresser, a plain woman of middle age, and Big
Abbey's other hoodlum. As they enter, the second hoodlum
is talking. Salome sits in one of the chairs, her face dull and
listless, her hands loose by her sides. She appears unaware of
what is said and done around her.

SECOND HOODLUM

(*to Salome*)
You can't do that. What the hell kind of jazz is that
—break a number, walk out—

BIG ABBEY

(*to second hoodlum, interrupting*)
Shut up!

SECOND HOODLUM

But, Boss, I was only trying—

BIG ABBEY

Get out!

The second hoodlum nods and starts toward the door.

BIG ABBEY

(*to the first hoodlum*)
You too. Out!

The first hoodlum exits.

DRESSER

I tried to talk to her, Big Abbey. She came running
in here and fell into that chair. Just like that. She
been sitting like that—

BIG ABBEY

All right. Get out.

The dresser exits.

BIG ABBEY

(*to Salome*)
Salome, listen to me—
(*Salome does not react.*)
Now listen! You hear me?

He turns to Joshua, who has been standing alongside the door since he entered, watching and listening.

BIG ABBEY

(*cont'd*)
You see that? That's the way she is—becomes a God-damn zombie. Go ahead, talk to her, miracle man.

JOSHUA

Leave us alone.

BIG ABBEY

What?

JOSHUA

I said, leave us alone. I can't help her if you're here.

Big Abbey stares at Joshua for a long moment. Then, baffled and angry, he exits. Joshua remains standing, watching Salome. As long an interval as possible goes by, before she turns her head to look at him. She stares at him. When she speaks, at the beginning, her tone is lifeless.

SALOME

Who are you?

JOSHUA

My name is Joshua. I'm a carpenter.

SALOME

Are you a friend of his?

JOSHUA

I have no enemies.

SALOME

Why did he call you miracle man?

JOSHUA

Some say that I work miracles.

SALOME

Do you?

JOSHUA

Sometimes—simple miracles.

SALOME

What do you mean?

JOSHUA

Like the miracle of love, or faith, or belief—

SALOME

(*the first note of life in her voice*)
What do you believe in? I believe in nothing.

JOSHUA

I know. Sometimes it is very hard to believe. But
sometimes I believe in men and in women—

SALOME

Do you believe in me?

JOSHUA

Yes, I believe in you.

SALOME

(*looking at her own body and aware of it*)
I'm naked—

JOSHUA

We're all naked, Salome.

Salome goes behind the screen, wraps a robe around her.
She is changed as she emerges.

SALOME

What did you do to me? I was all right until I saw
you out there.

JOSHUA

And when you saw me?

SALOME

(*with irritation*)
Who are you anyway? You don't look like anyone
to me. You look like a crumb. You a preacher? I got

no use for preachers. Go elsewhere, mister. Get off
my back. Go work your miracles. Leave me alone.

JOSHUA

(*nodding*)
All right.

He starts for the door, only a step away, puts his hand on
the knob. Salome is watching him, almost with desperation.

SALOME

Wait a minute, mister.
(*Joshua pauses, looking at her.*)

SALOME

(*cont'd*)
Why did Big Abbey bring you here?

JOSHUA

He thought I could help you.

SALOME

That lousy bastard—I can live without his help. And
without yours, mister.

JOSHUA

All right.

SALOME

What kind of help? You some kind of voodoo
doctor?

JOSHUA

No.

SALOME

Then how can you help me?

JOSHUA

I don't know. Sometimes, when the soul is sick, I can make it better.

SALOME

When the soul is sick! You break me up, miracle worker. You sure as hell break me up. Who told you I got a soul? Big Abbey?

JOSHUA

Big Abbey. You.

SALOME

Well, listen, mister. Go home and peddle your goods there. I got no soul. I threw it away the first time I saw my mother in the hay with a man. The first time I sold it for bread—the first time I plunged for kicks. I got no soul, I got no hope, and I don't believe in one God-damn thing. I got nothing, mister, nothing!

Her voice rises on this speech, and when she finishes, she covers her face with her hands and stands there, swaying, her body wracked with dry sobs. Then she moves almost blindly to the chaise and drops onto it, sitting. Her hands fall, and she stares at Joshua. He doesn't move.

SALOME

(*in a whisper*)
What's your name?

JOSHUA

Joshua.

SALOME

You told me before and I don't remember. I don't
want to remember anything. It just hurts when I remember. Oh, my God, it hurts so much—so much.
(*She rises, facing him.*)
Joshua—help me, help me—please, please help me—

52. INT. THE SHOP. MORNING

Joshua is alone in his shop, working at the bench, when
the outside door opens and Salome enters. She wears a fur
coat over a dark, long-sleeved dress.

She enters slowly, and moves toward the counter, her eyes
examining the place, the old furniture, the tools, the work-
benches. From her, CLOSE, we move to her POV and then—

CLOSE on Joshua.

JOSHUA

Good morning, Salome.
(*He smiles at her, as if it were perfectly natural
for her to come.*)

SALOME

(*her eyes still examining*)
This is where you work?

JOSHUA

My father and me—we work here, we live here, with
my mother and my cousin.

SALOME

You're just a carpenter—

JOSHUA

That's all, Salome. Just a carpenter.

SALOME

Last night, when I got home, I couldn't sleep. I
didn't want to sleep. It was like I had just awakened.
Do you know what I mean?

JOSHUA

I think so.

SALOME

I got dressed again, and I went out and walked. I
guess I walked for hours, and then I said to myself,
"I won't go back there. Not ever."
  (*Joshua watches her and waits.*)
It's not mine the place where I lived. It never was.
It's Big Abbey's.
  (*She pauses.*)
Joshua—can I stay here?

JOSHUA

If you wish to.

SALOME

Joshua, I love you. Don't say anything. I don't
want anything. Just let me love you.

JOSHUA

There's nothing bad in love, Salome.

SALOME

There's bad in me. You don't wash it out overnight,
Joshua. If I stay here, Big Abbey will come here.

JOSHUA

Then he'll come, Salome.

SALOME

You don't know him.

JOSHUA

I know him a little.

SALOME

And you're not afraid of him, Joshua?

JOSHUA

(*very slowly*)
I'm afraid of many things—more afraid than I am
of Big Abbey.

SALOME

Then I can stay?

As Salome speaks this last line, Mary enters from the apartment.

CLOSE on Mary, as Joshua turns.

JOSHUA

Mother, this is Salome. She has no place to go. She wants to stay here.

MARY

Poor child—
(*She goes to Salome.*)
You're trembling.

53. EXT. STREET. JOSHUA

As he walks down the street, his head bent against the wind.

54. EXT. THE STREET OF THE BANK

LONG ANGLE SHOT of Joshua as he turns into this street.

ANOTHER ANGLE as he walks slowly toward the bank but across the street from it.

CLOSE-UP on Joshua to set his POV.

55. EXT. THE BANK. JOSHUA'S POV

The bank as Joshua sees it. A few people going in and out. Then a car draws up to the curb outside the bank. In the car: Frankie, Joey, and Buttons.

56. EXT. THE CAR

CLOSE on the car as two of the boys get out. Joey remains at the wheel. Frankie has his hand in his coat pocket, clutching the gun. Buttons has both hands in his pockets. In one, a gun crudely carved out of wood. In the other, a brown paper bag.

CLOSE on Joshua, who watches. His face is twisted with pain.

MEDIUM CLOSE on the bank entrance as Frankie and Buttons enter.

57. INT. THE BANK

As the two boys enter.

There are half a dozen customers in the bank. At one side, the uniformed bank guard.

Frankie remains near the entrance, his hand in his pocket, gripping the gun.

Buttons walks to a teller's window. There is a woman behind the window.

CLOSE on the teller's face as Buttons takes the toy gun out of one pocket, the paper bag out of the other. He pushes the paper bag across to the woman. Panic on her face as he speaks.

BUTTONS

Lady, this is a stickup! Put the money from your drawer in that bag.

CLOSE on teller's face. Panic. Beginning of hysteria, but no response to demand.

BUTTONS

God-damn you, do what I say!
(*He is beginning to tremble with his own nerves.*)

CLOSE on Buttons as suddenly the alarm goes off. He starts like a frightened animal.

SWEEPING camera movement to the guard, going for his gun.

FULL on Buttons as he stands there, the toy gun in his hand. The sound of pistol shots, and his body ripped by the impact of the bullets.

SWEEP to guard, shooting deliberately at Buttons.

FULL on Frankie as he draws his gun, aims deliberately at the guard, and fires.

FULL on guard as he falls.

58. EXT. FRONT OF BANK

As Joshua enters. He stares for a moment at Frankie, who returns the look defiantly and then bolts through the door.

WIDE on guard and Buttons. The guard is dead, Buttons dying.

FULL on Joshua as he walks over to Buttons.

Now a small crowd has gathered around the two men, but no one makes any move to help Buttons. Joshua kneels beside him, lifts his head gently. Buttons looks at Joshua, a look of supplication and despair. Then he is dead.

Joshua picks up the crude, home-made imitation of a gun as he rises.

CLOSE on gun in Joshua's hands.

59. EXT. STREET

As Frankie and Joey, in the car, are cut off by a car cutting broadside in front of them. Three *ROMANS* leap out of the car and cover them.

The Romans are tall, strong, good-looking young men, erect in bearing and very military. They wear the uniforms of highway patrolmen, no insignia, but obviously police, whipcord breeches, Sam Browne belts, etc. Their car is a long, white sedan.

Two of the Romans carry tommy guns. The third, the *CENTURION*, wears a sidearm. This is belted low down on one leg. All three carry billies.

The two Romans cover the car with their guns. The Centurion flings open the door. When Frankie pulls back, the Centurion grabs him by the collar and drags him out. Joey follows of his own accord. Frankie gets to his feet, and the two stand there, covered by the guns. The Centurion frisks them and removes Frankie's gun.

CENTURION

(*holding the gun*)
Where did you get this?

FRANKIE

(*defiantly*)
Write me a letter, Daddy-O.

CENTURION

(*He hits Frankie suddenly with his open hand. The blow staggers Frankie.*)
Lousy punk! When I ask, answer! Where did you get the gun?

FRANKIE

(*trying to grin*)
Call me long distance, Daddy-O.

One of the Romans swings his tommy gun and smashes it against the back of Frankie's head. Frankie goes down and lies there on his face.

CENTURION

Take them both in. We'll sweat it out of them.

60. EXT. IN FRONT OF BANK

Joshua, confronted by the Centurion, who is backed by two of his Romans. A crowd stands around and watches.

As they talk, the bodies of the guard and Buttons are brought out of the bank and put in a black hearse.

CENTURION

How do you fit into this, mister?

JOSHUA

I don't know.

CENTURION

What's your name?

JOSHUA

Joshua.

CENTURION

Yes, the miracle worker. Is this one of your miracles? They tell me you knew the dead thief.

JOSHUA

I knew him, yes.

CENTURION

You keep strange company for a preacher. What
did he tell you when he died?

JOSHUA

Nothing. He died the way he lived, silently and
hopelessly.

CENTURION

Then you pity him, preacher?

JOSHUA

I pity him, yes—as I pity you—as I pity myself. We
share a common bondage, Centurion. We are all of
human flesh and blood. I envy those who can judge.
I never learned how.

CENTURION

It's not too late, miracle worker. I let you go this
time. But look for better company than thieves and
whores.

61. INT. THE SHOP

FULL on Joseph, who is working at his bench, and then his
POV:

FULL on Joshua, as he enters from street.

Joshua stands inside the door. His father watches him.
Joshua holds his hands in front of him, palms up, staring at
them. Then his hands drop. Slowly, with weariness, he moves
to the counter, takes off his coat, and picks up his work.

Now the outside door is flung open, and Big Abbey enters. He slams the door behind him, and confronts Joshua.

CLOSE on Joseph as Big Abbey speaks.

BIG ABBEY

Where is she?
(*in fury*)

JOSHUA

(*continuing with his work*)
She's here.

BIG ABBEY

You play hard, preacher. You play with dynamite. You sure as hell pile up trouble for yourself.

Joshua continues to work, bent over the bench. Big Abbey strides around the counter and reaches out, as to grab Joshua's shirt front.

CLOSE-UP on Joshua's face as he looks up to confront Big Abbey—who stops his own movement, stares at Joshua. Their eyes meet. Big Abbey turns away, then back.

BIG ABBEY

Where is she?

JOSHUA

I told you she's here. She came here. I don't turn away people who come here. Not even you, Big Abbey.

BIG ABBEY

She's coming back with me. Tell her that!

JOSHUA

I give no orders, Big Abbey. She's inside with my
cousin and my mother. She came of her own will, and
she can go of her own will. It's her decision to make,
not mine.

Big Abbey glares at Joshua. Then he swings around and
strides through to the apartment in back of the shop.

FULL on Joshua, who stands looking at the curtain through
which Big Abbey passed.

WIDE on back of shop, Joseph watching Joshua.

62.   INT. KITCHEN

The three women are in the kitchen as Big Abbey enters.
We pick him up.

CLOSE, as he stands in the doorway, and then his *POV*:

WIDE, the small kitchen, Sarah washing dishes, Salome dry-
ing them, and Mary mincing an apple as part of the Passover
preparation. They stop in their work, turn to face him.

BIG ABBEY

(*to Salome*)
Just what in hell do you think you're doing here?

SALOME

Don't talk like that here.

BIG ABBEY

What in hell is this—a God-damn shrine? I talk as I
please!

Mary and Sarah watching with growing alarm. This is another world that has pushed into their kitchen. But Salome's
temper rises. She takes a quick step and slaps Big Abbey hard
across the face.

SALOME

Not here, you pig! Not here! You don't use that lan-
guage here! You don't shout here!

BIG ABBEY

Now listen! I took enough from you! You're coming with me!

SALOME

I am not coming with you. Not now. Not ever.

BIG ABBEY

All right. You want it the hard way—

He starts toward her. Mary moves over, next to Salome,
protectively.

CROSS SHOT FULL from reverse of previous and opposite
entrance to kitchen. We see them all now, from our shooting vantage behind sink and table.

Behind Big Abbey, who has entered the kitchen, Joshua at
doorway.

JOSHUA

Big Abbey.

His voice is cold and hard, neither threatening nor excited, but with implicit power. Big Abbey halts and turns to face the doorway.

JOSHUA

(*cont'd*)
Don't use force in this house, Big Abbey.

BIG ABBEY

I could break you in two, carpenter.

JOSHUA

But you won't, Big Abbey. You know that you won't, and I know it. You spoke to the woman. You heard her answer. That's all, Big Abbey. Go now.

Once again, Big Abbey glares his hatred, and once again his will breaks against Joshua's. He turns to look at Salome again, and then he stalks past Joshua and out.

63. INT. THE SHOP

As Big Abbey pushes through the curtain and across the shop to the door.

CLOSE on Joseph, and to Big Abbey as Joseph's POV.
Big Abbey exits.

64. EXT. THE FRONT OF THE SHOP

As Big Abbey exits, and then stands a moment.

CLOSE on his face, and then from his POV, CARIOT.

FULL SHOT of Cariot, gray business suit, shoes shined, white collar, white tie, steel-rimmed glasses, the clerk, the white-collar man full of piousness, a pious face and demeanor, his hands clasped in front of him.

CARIOT

Big Abbey?

BIG ABBEY

(*turning on him*)
Who the hell are you?

CARIOT

You are not the only one he betrayed.
(*Big Abbey studies Cariot through narrowed eyes.*)
My name is Cariot. I am one of his followers.

BIG ABBEY

So you're one of his followers. So what?

CARIOT

I can help you.

BIG ABBEY

You? Little man, you make me laugh.

CARIOT

I'm not laughing, Big Abbey. I believed in what he preached. But he betrayed what he preached.

BIG ABBEY

The hell with what he preached!

CARIOT

Then I'm wasting my time?

BIG ABBEY

All right, little man. You got a proposition—make it!

CARIOT

I can sell him, and there are those who will buy—
(*He begins to walk. Big Abbey falls in step with him.*)

TWO SHOT. TRUCKING

CARIOT

(*cont'd*)
I'm a hard-working man. I'm a poor man.

BIG ABBEY

How do I know you'll deliver?

CARIOT

From what I hear, you know how to deal with those who don't deliver.

BIG ABBEY

(*grinning*)
You hear right, little man. What's your price?

CARIOT

Three hundred dollars.

BIG ABBEY

(*laughing*)
Knock it off, little man. I can pay my boys to handle
him—for one tenth of that.
(*He reaches into his pocket and takes out a roll of
bills.*)
Thirty bucks—take it or leave it.

Cariot stops walking to stare at Big Abbey. He hesitates
for a long moment. Then he nods and takes the money.

65. EXT. FRONT OF GROCERY

As Mary enters. A plain, old-fashioned grocery and vege-
table store in the neighborhood. The windows are piled with
boxes of matzos for the Passover. Inside, geese hang from
hooks.

Mary wears a large shawl against the cold. She carries an
oilcloth shopping bag.

66. INT. THE GROCERY

REVERSE OF 65. As Mary enters.

FULL SHOT of grocery's interior. A man behind the counter
waits on the two women who are already there when Mary
enters. The grocery man is middle-aged, of the nature of his
trade.

One of the women is Mrs. Marat. The other is simply a
customer, loquacious, the mother of children, quicker with
speech than with thought.

During the first few moments after she enters, Mary goes
about selecting some of the things she wants, two boxes of
the matzos, some horseradish roots from a pile in a box, etc.
Then the conversation impinges.

CUSTOMER

All I'm telling you, Mrs. Marat, is what I heard.
And those who saw it, saw it.

STOREKEEPER

Will you need some eggs, Mrs. Marat? I have them
fresh for the Passover.

MRS. MARAT

Please. I'll take six.
  (*to the customer*)
I don't say you're lying. I wouldn't say anything like
that. It's so hard to believe. It frightens you. And I
know Joshua. I know him.

With Joshua's name in the conversation, Mary's attention
is caught. As yet, Mrs. Marat has not noticed her. Mary
stands behind the two customers.

STOREKEEPER

Here are the eggs, Mrs. Marat. And I'll tell you
something. Where there's a fire, there's smoke. Ain't
nobody been in here today but said something about
that child.

CUSTOMER

There you are! Now maybe you'll believe me, Mrs.
Marat.

MRS. MARAT

I didn't say I didn't believe you.

CUSTOMER

All right, then. What I heard was this. He actually raised the child from the dead. The doctor had examined her, and pronounced her dead. You can't tell me a doctor don't know what he's talking about—

CLOSE on Mary as she listens.

—and he says she was dead. Well, that's good enough for me. Then Joshua come into the bedroom with Jairus. He pulls back the sheet. She ain't dead, she sleeps, Joshua says. Then Joshua kisses her. Then the child opens her eyes and sits up, spry and alive as can be—

MARY

(*interrupting desperately*)
No! No! It's not true. It's not true. Why do you say such things? Why?

The two women and the storekeeper stare at her, speechless and amazed.

67. EXT. STREET

TRUCKING SHOT CLOSE on Mary as she hurries through the streets in the fading later-afternoon light. She carries the heavy shopping bag, stuffed with food for the Passover. Her face reflects worry and fear.

68. INT. THE SHOP

As Mary enters. Joshua is not there. Joseph is at his worktable.

CLOSE on Mary as she enters.

CLOSE on Joseph as he sees her, his face stern and unhappy.

JOSEPH

A house unblessed on the Passover eve—

MARY

No! No—this house is blessed.

JOSEPH

With what? How does your son bless it? With
magic? With thieves? With prostitutes?

MARY

With love. With gentleness. With forgiveness.

JOSEPH

Is that all God asks of a man? Love? Forgiveness? I
tell you this—my house has been turned into a den
of thieves and prostitutes.

MARY

Joseph, tonight is Passover—

JOSEPH

Not in this house. Not for me.

MARY

You don't mean that. You can't mean that. A house
without Passover tonight is like a day without the
sun.

Joseph lays aside his tools. He takes his coat from the peg
where it hangs, and then his hat.

MARY

Where are you going?

JOSEPH

To those who keep Passover instead of destroying it.

MARY

Your son will be here.
   (*pleadingly*)
Don't leave us tonight, Joseph—I beg you not to
leave us tonight.

JOSEPH

Your son will keep Passover his way, and I'll keep it
my way.

He starts toward the door. As he opens it, Mary cries out
after him.

MARY

Joseph—please!

He exits.

Mary stares after him for a long moment. Then she drops
into a chair, her face twisted with grief. Then, with a long
sigh, she rises, picks up her shopping bag, and goes through
the curtain at the back of the store.

69.   INTERIOR. DINING ROOM

REVERSE OF 68, as Mary emerges from the curtain, goes
through the dining room, and into the kitchen.

70. INT. KITCHEN

FULL SHOT as Mary enters. Sarah and Salome are there, preparing food for the Passover. They sit at the little work-table, Salome cleaning carrots, Sarah carefully pulling the small feathers out of a goose.

Mary wearily puts her shopping bag on the counter.

SARAH

You brought the matzos?

Mary nods wearily.

We'll need them. They'll all be here—Cariot and Peter and Andrew and the rest—with Uncle, four-teen at the table. Salome will help us. Salome bought this bird. It was good of her—

SALOME

It was nothing. For the kindness in this house.

MARY

No—

SARAH

What is it?

MARY

There's no kindness in this house now. Your uncle won't be here for the Passover.

SARAH

(*rising*)
No. No, he wouldn't do that.

MARY

He went away—

SARAH

Why? Why?

MARY

Because his heart is filled with frustration at Joshua.
I don't know what is happening. I don't understand
it. At the grocery, they were talking about Joshua—
that he raised a girl from the dead. Jairus's daughter.

SARAH

He told me. She wasn't dead. She slept. Joshua
awakened her.

MARY

And the doctor?

SARAH

Doctors make mistakes.

SALOME

You're his mother. Could he do something evil?
Could he?

MARY

No. He could not.

SALOME

Do you think it's good to worship death? I wor-
shiped death—and it was life Joshua gave me, love

for what is alive, not what is dead. Why is it wrong
for him to set himself against death?

MARY

Because only God—not any man—only God can
raise the dead.

SARAH

And isn't that what Joshua said to Jairus? Joshua
knew the child wasn't dead. Aunt Mary, he knew it.

MARY

I'm so afraid. I was so cold coming here—like a skin
of darkness and fear drawn over the whole earth.
And now Joseph goes away—

SALOME

He'll come back. Mary, he'll come back.

71. INT. THE DINING ROOM

This is the *Seder*, the Feast of Passover, the night of the
Last Supper.

A white linen cloth has been spread over the long table in
the dining room. Joshua sits at the head of the table, in an
armchair that is bolstered with pillows.

On the long benches that flank the table, the followers of
Joshua, the disciples, are seated. It is important that Joshua
should be flanked by Cariot and Peter, the fisherman. The
seating of the other ten may be at the discretion of the di-
rector.

The three women, Mary, Sarah, and Salome, will serve the
table and thereby not be seated.

The table is set with plain dishes, but there is an attempt at all the splendor that this poor home can provide. There are two seven-branched candlesticks. There are four plates piled high with matzos, the matzos covered with linen napkins. In front of each plate, a goblet for wine, plain glass and cheap but simple and pleasant in shape. A deep platter contains hard-boiled eggs in salt water. Another dish contains bitter herb. Another, a mixture of chopped apple and raisins.

Joshua and the disciples are dressed as we have seen them, Joshua in his brown shirt and work pants, Peter in his fisherman's sweater, Cariot in his suit, shirt, and tie, ANDREW in his work clothes—and the others at the discretion of the costumer. All of them, however, wear skull caps, and Joshua wears, as a scarf around his shoulders, a beautiful silk *tallith*.

FULL SHOT of room and table, as Salome and Sarah enter. Each carries a bottle of red wine. Joshua's glass is filled first —then the others' as the two women move down the table.

Mary enters, stands unobtrusively beside the kitchen door.

CLOSE on Mary's face, so that we follow her *POV*.

CLOSE on Joshua, as he slowly rises, the wine goblet in his hand, and then back from him with—

INTERCUTS CLOSE as he speaks.

JOSHUA

Blessed is the fruit of the earth on the Passover—

THE DISCIPLES

Amen.

JOSHUA

Blessed is the Passover, for we were slaves in Egypt, and now we are free.

THE DISCIPLES

(*softly*)
Amen.

JOSHUA

We were oppressed, and now we lift our heads.

THE DISCIPLES

Amen.

JOSHUA

It was dark then, and now it is light.

THE DISCIPLES

Amen.

JOSHUA

Blessed is the Lord of the Universe, my Father in heaven, who makes the sun to shine and clothes the night in darkness.

THE DISCIPLES

Amen.

INTERCUT through above and what follows to the faces of the disciples, to the faces of the women.

When they have finished pouring the wine, Sarah and Salome put down the bottles on the table, move back, and watch until Joshua finishes the blessing.

JOSHUA

Who makes us to see when we are blind.

THE DISCIPLES

Amen.

JOSHUA

To hear when we are deaf—

THE DISCIPLES

Amen.

JOSHUA

To smile when our hearts are broken—

THE DISCIPLES

Amen.

JOSHUA

To pity when our hearts are hardened—

THE DISCIPLES

Amen.

CLOSE on Cariot for the above "amen" and following "amen." His lips do not move.

INTERCUT on Joshua, who notices this.

JOSHUA

And to love—out of all our suffering, to love and not to hate—

THE DISCIPLES

Amen.

JOSHUA

For He gave us the Passover, and He turned our
faces away from bondage, and we will remember this,
indeed forever—

THE DISCIPLES

Amen.

JOSHUA

Wherefor we eat the matzo, the bread of affliction,
and we drink the red wine, the color of the blood
of the innocent—

Joshua raises his glass now.

Baruch atah Adonoi Elohano Melek Haolum boray
pre hagaufin—

He drinks.

THE DISCIPLES

Amen.

They drink.
Joshua sinks back into his chair. Mary and the women
go into the kitchen.

CARIOT

(*to Andrew, who sits beside him*)
He makes his own Passover.

ANDREW

So long as he makes it holy.

Joshua meanwhile has uncovered the plate of matzos in front of him, and now he passes a piece of matzo to each of the disciples. As he gives his piece to Cariot:

JOSHUA

No amen from you, Cariot? Do I worship so poorly?

CARIOT

(*uneasily*)
Not poorly, Joshua—but strangely, I think.

JOSHUA

Strangely? I don't think so, Cariot. I thanked God and I praised man. Is that so strange?

CARIOT

Are you the son of God?

JOSHUA

No. No, Cariot. I'm the son of man. That's enough, I think.

Mary, Salome, and Sarah begin to put the food on the table, the roast goose, the vegetables.

Peter, sitting opposite Cariot and next to Joshua, carves the goose.

PETER

I follow you, Joshua. There's no man I look at with the respect I look at you, Joshua. No man!

JOSHUA

And now you're disturbed, Peter. Because I serve
God strangely?

PETER

Because I don't understand what you do—so help
me, I don't, Joshua. With thieves, murderers, gang
leaders—

ANDREW

You went with Big Abbey. Do you deny that,
Joshua?

CARIOT

You knew the thieves would rob and kill—

PETER

And you brought Big Abbey's woman here, a slut,
a prostitute, a woman of evil ways.

CLOSE on Salome who hears this and reacts accordingly—
frozen where she stands, her face full of horror.

JOSHUA

There she stands, behind you, Peter. Her name
is Salome. Look at her and tell me how evil she is!

CARIOT

How can we tell you, Joshua, when you have become
the only judge of what is good and what is evil?

JOSHUA

I judge no one. Who am I to judge?
(*The harsh edge leaves his voice. It becomes gentle.*)
Do I wear the robes of a judge? I'm a carpenter—
with the small gift to heal a human soul when it's
sick, and I teach what I know of love and kindness.
(*He shakes his head.*)
This is the Passover. Why do you accuse me on the
Passover?

Salome, moving blindly, goes into the kitchen. Sarah
follows her.

INTERCUT: THE KITCHEN. Salome stands there, tears
running down her face. Sarah tries to comfort her.

SALOME

Why do they torture him like that?

SARAH

I don't know—I don't know.

71.   (*cont'd*)

THE DINING ROOM:

CARIOT

Forgive us, Joshua, if we feel that you have betrayed
things we believe in—

JOSHUA

(*looking at Cariot strangely*)
All men betray the things they love.

CARIOT

Why do you look at me like that?

JOSHUA

With pity, Cariot—

At the other end of the table, the soft hum of a Passover song rises.

CLOSE on the faces of the disciples at the other end, as the song builds up, but always muted.

The motion of food being eaten, wine goblets lifted and tilted.

A NOTE ON 71: Throughout this scene of the Passover, a chiaroscuro effect should be sought, deep shadows in the background and facial lighting strongly defined, the flicker of candlelight and a constant, searching movement of the camera. I have made no attempt to indicate the angles, but the play of angle and light should be constant, nervous and implicit with foreboding.

Against this, as we cut out of the scene, the song is light, gay, and lilting.

72. INT. THE SHOP

As the Passover guests leave, Joshua stands there, bidding them good night. The last to leave is Peter.

Peter halts in front of Joshua. Suddenly, he takes Joshua's hand.

JOSHUA

Make no pledges, Peter.

PETER

Why, Master? Why?

JOSHUA

And now you call me master? Peter, if I taught you anything, leave it that way.

PETER

I'll never betray you. I'll never turn my back on you.

JOSHUA

(*smiling at him*)
Fisherman—go and sleep. It's late.

Now the door to the shop opens, and Joseph enters, tired, worn. He takes a few steps inside and stands looking at Joshua and Peter.

Peter goes past him and exits.

73. EXT. THE FRONT OF THE SHOP

REVERSE OF 72 as Peter leaves the shop. It is nighttime. Peter takes a few steps, and then, from his *POV:*

Cariot, a figure in the dark.

PETER

(*recognizing him*)
Cariot?

Cariot turns to face him.

PETER

(*cont'd*)
You're waiting for someone?

CARIOT

No. Only thinking.

PETER

Will you walk with me?

CARIOT

I must walk with my own thoughts.

PETER

Oh? Then I'll say good night.

CARIOT

Good night, Peter.

Cariot turns and walks off.

CLOSE on Peter. Then Peter's *POV* on Cariot.

74.   EXT. STREET (Night)

The journey of Cariot through the streets to his betrayal of Joshua, a succession of angles to build the mood necessary for the scene of the actual betrayal.

LONG SHOTS from rooftop to spot the single image on empty streets, the hurrying image of Cariot as his own demons pursue him.

CLOSE to reveal Cariot's struggle with himself.

FULL under lamplight, as Cariot pauses, frozen in his own fear.

Such in general as the man moves.

75.   EXT. THE TEMPLE

SAME AS 20. First from the Temple steps as Cariot pauses there, and then Cariot's *POV*:

WIDE, the Temple. Then back and

WIDER, as we see the whole front of the Temple, Cariot standing in front of the steps, small, a figure of fear and loneliness in the night.

Then Cariot mounts the steps and opens the door of the Temple.

76. INT. THE TEMPLE

A large room, at least sixty feet long and forty feet wide. A bare room, such a room as is used for lodge meetings. At either side, chairs against the wall. Strange lighting.

REVERSE OF 75, as Cariot enters and closes the door behind him. Then he turns, and we see the length of the room from his *POV*, thus:

To the end of the room, where the three *JUDGES* sit. They sit behind a table. Candles burn on the table. Books, large books in black bindings, lie open upon the table.

The Judges are old men. They wear clerical collars, for they are also priests. They wear long scholastic robes. They look at Cariot silently as he stands there, watching them.

Cariot knows that this moment of betrayal echoes and re-echoes down through all the ages. Fear such as he experiences now cannot be described. His whole being is fear, but having taken his initial steps, he cannot retreat. He walks toward the Judges, the camera facing him,

TRUCKING ahead of him, and then *CUTTING* to his *POV*,

FULL ON THE JUDGES, and then,

WIDE AND ABOVE, back the full length and height of the room, so that we see Cariot in the distance, small as he stands before the Judges.

FIRST JUDGE

Who are you?

CARIOT

Cariot. I am Cariot.

SECOND JUDGE

Why do you come here, Cariot?

CARIOT

My conscience brings me.

CLOSE, THREE SHOT ON JUDGES.

FIRST JUDGE

Into the holy of holies on this holy night?

CARIOT

Shall a righteous man wait for tomorrow?

SECOND JUDGE

Who named you Cariot the Righteous?

CARIOT

My conscience.

THIRD JUDGE

Always your conscience, mister.
    (*Cariot stands with head bowed.*)
Raise your head, sir! Let us see the man instead of
the conscience!
    (*Cariot raises his head.*)

Look at us! Open your eyes, man! I want to see what comes with the conscience into the holy of holies.

FIRST JUDGE

I know the face.

SECOND JUDGE

Why is a righteous man afraid, Cariot?

THIRD JUDGE

I also know the face. Who are you, Cariot?

CARIOT

A follower of Joshua, the carpenter.

THIRD JUDGE

He who preaches on the hill?

CARIOT

Yes.

THIRD JUDGE

He sent you here?

CARIOT

(*after a tortured moment*)
No. I came of my own will—to denounce him.

THIRD JUDGE

Of your own will. And tell me, Cariot, why couldn't it wait until the holy days are over? Why do you come here on the night of the Passover?

CARIOT

He defames the Passover.

FIRST JUDGE

How does he defame it, Cariot? Does he deny it?

CARIOT

No.

FIRST JUDGE

Does he eat of leavened bread?

CARIOT

No. He blasphemes.

SECOND JUDGE

How does he blaspheme, Cariot?

CARIOT

He speaks with God's voice.

THIRD JUDGE

And whose voice do you speak with, Cariot? Who gave you your conscience?

CARIOT

(*desperately*)
He raises the dead!

There is a long moment of silence now.

THIRD JUDGE

Here in this holy place, Cariot, speak only the truth.

CARIOT

I swear that—

FIRST JUDGE

(*interrupting harshly*)
Don't swear here, Cariot. Whom did he raise from
the dead?

CARIOT

The daughter of Jairus.

THIRD JUDGE

Was there witness?

CARIOT

There was.

THIRD JUDGE

We have our own ways of finding the truth, Cariot.
And let me tell you this. If you come here bringing
false witness in this holy place, then may God have
mercy on your soul, not his.
(*He stretches out an arm, directing his finger
at Cariot.*)
Now, go with your conscience, Cariot!

Back now for

LONG FULL SHOT from doorway to temple, down length of room, as Cariot shrinks away from the three judges, backs away from them step by step, then turns and almost runs to the door.

77. EXT. FRONT OF TEMPLE

As Cariot emerges into the night and goes down the steps of the temple. He takes a few steps, then pauses, and turns and from his *POV*:

FULL on the front of the temple.

78. EXT. STREET

Cariot walks; he runs a few steps; he stands panting; he looks about him in terror; he girds himself and walks through the night like a man dragging his feet through quicksand.

Then, a voice from the night:

PETER

Cariot!

Cariot halts. He turns slowly.

You still wander in the night, Cariot?

CARIOT

I walk with my thoughts.

PETER

As I do. I'll walk with you, Cariot.

He falls into place beside Cariot.

TWO SHOT trucking in front of them.

PETER

I couldn't sleep. No fishing boats sail tomorrow, so
I'll walk, I told myself. Wherever I walk, I am not
lost, and if a man comes out of the night, my heart
warms to him. I'm not afraid. Since I met Joshua,
I have never been afraid. It's hard for me to put into
words. Do you know what I mean, Cariot?

CLOSE on Cariot's face. He nods.

79. INT. THE SHOP

The first light of dawn the following morning. In the shop
it is still dim, shadowed. Joshua enters from the curtained
doorway, from the apartment.

He stands silently at first, a dark, shadowed figure. Then
he goes to his workbench. He picks up one tool, then another, handles them gently, with love, turns them over, feels
them, then replaces them.

He walks to the peg where his coat hangs, takes it down,
and puts it on. Then he goes to the outside door, opens it,
and passes through.

80. EXT. FRONT OF SHOP

REVERSE OF 79 as Joshua emerges on the street. Very early
dawn, the street still in shadow, the lightening sky above.

Joshua stands in the street in front of the shop, his back
to the shop. He breathes deeply, savoring the air as if he were
drinking wine. His face is full of the repose and joy of being
alive on this fine morning.

Across Joshua to the door of the shop as Mary emerges.

MARY

Joshua.

JOSHUA

Mother—
(*He turns to her.*)
It's a cold morning, Mother.

MARY

You haven't slept. It's so early, Joshua—

JOSHUA

I'm not tired, Mother.

MARY

Your father's still asleep, Joshua. It took a long time
for him to sleep. He's disturbed. And then, when
he slept, he tossed and turned—

JOSHUA

(*going over to her and placing his hands on her
cheeks*)
You worry about everyone but yourself. You stay
awake and watch whether others sleep.

MARY

Be kind to him, Joshua. He loves you.

JOSHUA

He's so afraid. How can I teach him not to be afraid?
He's my father.

MARY

And everyone else you can teach to be without fear.
You have nothing for your father.

JOSHUA

I have all the world for him. I don't know how to
give it to him—and he doesn't know how to take it.

MARY

I'll make coffee, Joshua. Come inside.

JOSHUA

In a little while, Mother. Look!
(*He points across the street where the first rays
of the sun strike the top of a building.*)
It's beautiful, isn't it? Everything this morning, the
way the air tastes, like good wine, that first light
of the sunrise. There's a whisper of the world coming
awake, but full of joy, Mother—and for a little
while, we're free and filled with love—

MARY

Come inside, Joshua.

JOSHUA

Soon, Mother, soon.
(*He kisses her.*)
Go inside now. It's cold.

Mary enters the shop, Joshua's *POV*. Then, as Joshua turns
back to the street, from his *POV*:

WIDE ON STREET AND PANNING as the disciples
move slowly and unhurriedly to join him.
(Specifically, at this moment, no music and no sound
except the rustle of footsteps in the crisp winter air. This to
be *noted for the scoring*, silence until the disciples are gathered
around Joshua.)

81. EXT. THE ENTIRE STREET

The twelve disciples are spread as they come to give their morning greeting to Joshua. Some approach from across the street, some from the side of the street where the shop is. Those across the street cross over toward Joshua at uneven intervals. Their movements are slow.

One by one, they come up to Joshua. Nothing is said. He greets them with a nod or a slight smile, and they form a group around him.

Only one holds back. This is Cariot. He remains outside the group, and we pick him up in Joshua's *POV*:

CLOSE on Cariot.

JOSHUA

Cariot!

Cariot remains where he is, looking at Joshua. Then Joshua moves toward him. Cariot takes a step away.

CARIOT

What is it?

JOSHUA

(*shaking his head*)
So afraid, Cariot. Always sensitive, afraid—so easily hurt. We have nothing to be afraid of, Cariot. We do no wrong. We take a human being's hand in brotherhood. That isn't wrong. Forgotten, perhaps, these days—but wrong? No. It's not wrong. The whole world is like a clenched fist of pain, but we bring pain to no one. So why should we be afraid? What should we fear?

Cariot doesn't answer. He continues to stare at Joshua, and now the *background silence* is broken.

Screaming sirens!

LONG AND WIDE to the end of the street, as two of the white cars that we saw in 59 appear in the distance, roar down the street, and come to a screeching stop in front of the shop. The doors are flung open and the Centurion and eight Romans leap out. As in 59, the Romans carry tommy guns.

But before the cars stop, the disciples break and begin to run. They run in wild, thoughtless, senseless fear toward both ends of the block. The Romans ignore them.

Only one disciple does not run. This is Cariot. Fixed by Joshua's stare, he remains where he is as the Romans surround them.

Then Cariot lifts one shaking hand and points to Joshua.

Two of the Romans sling their tommy guns over their shoulders and seize Joshua. He tears loose and turns on the Centurion.

JOSHUA

What is this? Am I a thief that you come at me this way with your guns and your hired thugs?
(*fiercely at the two Romans*)
Keep your hands off me!
(*They stand back, momentarily cowed by the force of his personality and cold anger. Then, to the Centurion:*)
What do you want?

CENTURION

Are you the carpenter, Joshua?

JOSHUA

Yes, my name is Joshua.

CENTURION

(*to Cariot*)
He's the one?

CARIOT

(*unable to face Joshua*)
Yes. Yes—him.

CENTURION

(*to Joshua*)
Come with us.
(*He points to the car.*)

Joshua stares at Cariot, who avoids his eyes at first, but then must turn and meet Joshua's look. A moment thus. Then Joshua walks over to the first white car and gets in the back, a Roman on each side of him.

ON CARIOT'S FACE when their eyes meet, and then Cariot's POV—to Joshua entering the car.

The Romans get into the cars. The motors are started and the cars begin to move. Then on:

THE FRONT OF THE SHOP

As Mary and Joseph and Sarah and Salome emerge. They look with silent horror at the two white cars pulling away, and then their POV shifts to:

CLOSE-UP of Cariot.

82. EXT. STREET

A street of tall, glass-front, modernistic office buildings. It is still very early morning, and the streets are empty, or almost empty, as the two white cars speed down and then come to a screeching stop in front of one of these buildings.

83. EXT. FRONT OF OFFICE BUILDING

FULL SHOT against office building as the Romans leap out of the white cars, form around Joshua, and march him into the office building. The Centurion leads them.

84. INT. OFFICE BUILDING LOBBY

REVERSE of above, as the Centurion, the Romans, and Joshua enter the building. Joshua is surrounded by the Romans, who walk with their tommy guns at ready.

The lobby is big, impressive, and modern, with expensive marble walls and floor.

BACK AND FULL to show procession through lobby to the elevator, and then

CLOSE on elevator as its doors open and the Romans and Joshua enter. Then the doors close.

85. INT. HALLWAY IN BUILDING, ON ELEVATOR DOOR

DIRECT CUT from 84, as elevator arrives, door opens, and the Centurion, Romans, and Joshua emerge.

86. INT. HALLWAY

TRUCKING SHOT down the hallway, and then *ANOTHER ANGLE* as Joshua is marched toward a specific door.

87. INT. DOOR TO PILATE'S OFFICE

The door is impressive. On it, in black letters, one word:

PROCURATOR

The Centurion swings back the door, and the Romans enter in two lines, Joshua between them.

88. INT. THE OFFICE OF PONTIUS PILATE

This is a magnificent office in the modern decor. As impressive as it is, the taste is excellent, and there is no note of cheapness or vulgarity in the furnishings.

The floor is white vinyl, the windows shaded with modern blinds, the walls white in some places, pastel shades in other places. There are handsome modern paintings on the walls, all nonobjective, and the few pieces of metallic sculpture are also in the modern vein. The chairs are modern and comfortable, black against the white background. Pilate's desk is topped with a great slab of white marble. The lighting is soft and indirect.

PILATE sits behind his desk. He is a man of middle age, handsome, sure of himself, utterly possessed and civilized in his manner, and urbane and controlled in his speech.

He wears a dark suit, beautifully cut, white shirt, dark silk tie. His hands rest on the desk, and during the scene he plays idly but not compulsively with a small brass ornament, a brass rod with a small eagle at one end.

At each side of the room, that is, to the left and right of Pilate sits a woman. One is *CLAUDIA*. The other is *HELEN*.

Claudia and Helen are dressed more or less alike, so a description of one will do for both.

Helen is a handsome, aristocratic-looking woman. She sits in a modern chair of black leather, her legs crossed. A coat of blond mink has been casually dropped from her shoulders, and it hangs over the back of the chair. She wears a beautiful, designer-type dress, long gloves, high-heeled alligators, and a large alligator purse. A diamond necklace and diamond earrings. She wears a handsome blond wig.

Much the same with Claudia. Wealth, luxury, indolence, and the thoughtless possession of all these.

Both women are tall and shapely.

As Joshua is brought into this room by the Romans, they open up away from him, leaving him in front of the desk. The Centurion presents himself at one side, facing Pilate.

PILATE

This is the man, Centurion?

CENTURION

Yes, sir. The carpenter, Joshua.

PILATE

He doesn't look very dangerous, Centurion.

CENTURION

No, sir.

PILATE

Did he make any difficulties for you?

CENTURION

Hardly, sir.

PILATE

(*with a soft touch of sarcasm*)
I think you can safely leave him here, Centurion.

CENTURION

He has a reputation for miracles, sir.

PILATE

So many of us do. And so rarely is it deserved, Centurion. I suggest that you and your men wait outside.

CENTURION

Very well, sir.

The Centurion goes to the outer door and holds it open. The Romans file through. Then he follows and closes the door behind him.

Meanwhile, Joshua stands there, looking at Pilate.

PILATE

So you are the carpenter, Joshua. Do you really work miracles?

JOSHUA

No, sir. Not in your sense.

PILATE

Oh? And what is my sense?

JOSHUA

The miracle that can't be explained. Magic—spells and such nonsense.

PILATE

Joshua, you disappoint me. Like all miracle workers who mix up a great, heady bowl of belief, one discovers that all they really sell is the fact that the hand is quicker than the eye.

JOSHUA

Perhaps.

PILATE

Yet they say you raised up one from the dead—

JOSHUA

No! I did not!

PILATE

Yet there's a miracle I would not resent. As a matter of fact, it would be useful to have someone like yourself around at an appropriate moment. Of course, one would want discretion. You could brew the devil's own mess by raising the dead at random. One of the few consolations we live with is the fact that the dead remain dead. You would not want to deprive us of that, would you, Joshua?

During the above and what follows, Claudia and Helen react with half interest and boredom. They use their compacts, renew their makeup, and pat their hair into place.

JOSHUA

I don't raise the dead.

PILATE

Whether you do or you don't, Joshua, is a matter for
the priests to bicker about. My own interest in you
lies elsewhere. But what miracles do you do?

JOSHUA

I don't *do* miracles. But sometimes I can make
people aware of a miracle that exists.

PILATE

Yes? And that?

JOSHUA

The miracle of love.

PILATE

Of course.

Here, the interest of Claudia and Helen is caught.

CLOSE on their faces.

PILATE

(*cont'd*)
Of course. But that's the most dangerous miracle
of all, isn't it?

JOSHUA

Yes—I suppose the sweetness of life is dangerous.

PILATE

And is it true, Joshua, that you tell people to love
each other as themselves?

JOSHUA

Yes. That's true.

PILATE

And they heed you. That's the rub of it. If you simply preached love and they paid you no mind, why then you'd simply be another philosopher. We've learned to live with the philosophers. The devil pops out when people stop hating each other.
(*Pilate shakes his head, and then opens a folder on his desk. He stares at the contents thoughtfully.*)
There is also this—if you are struck on one cheek, then it is better to turn the other cheek than to strike back. You preach that?

JOSHUA

I preach that.

PILATE

Well, really, isn't it contrary to human nature?

JOSHUA

To your nature, sir. Not to mine.

PILATE

That is the very devil, Joshua. Suppose there were enough like you. It wouldn't do, would it? We maintain half a million men under arms. What a bedlam there'd be if they began to turn the other cheek! We couldn't have it—too much at stake. The world is ours, you know.

CLOSE on Joshua, as he smiles slightly.

PILATE

(cont'd)
You disagree?

JOSHUA

I think the world is God's sir—not yours, not mine.

PILATE

Oh, come, come now! We are neither of us simple, Joshua. One does reverence to the gods—it's the decent, civilized thing to do. In our own great city, there are hundreds of temples. We have the gods of every nation on earth residing there in comfort and security. But just between us, the gods do precious little to assert their ownership of anything. It always helps to have a few regiments of well-trained fighting men, not to mention the proper weapons.
(He glances at the folder again.)
According to this, Joshua—you preach against the government, against authority—

JOSHUA

When people ask me about the government, I tell them to render to the government what belongs to the government and to God what belongs to God.

PILATE

You are a stubborn man, aren't you? And you do make the devil's own mess of your own case. You leave very little indeed to the government when you draw a line and say such and such belongs to us, and such and such belongs to God. You can't run an empire that way, Joshua.

(*His voice hardens now.*)

We don't share our subjects with God or gods. All belongs to us, life, honor, body, and soul!

Claudia stretches and yawns.

CLAUDIA

Really, this is a bore.

HELEN

(*looking at her watch*)
It's so late.

CLAUDIA

You said we'd be amused. I'm really not amused at all.

PILATE

(*to Claudia*)
Be patient, my dear.

CLAUDIA

Be patient, be patient. I'm tired of being patient. I'm tired of being bored.

PILATE

(*to Joshua*)
That doesn't leave us much choice, does it? They're both quite beautiful and quite frivolous. But then,

what am I to do with you, Joshua? Am I to be re-
membered as the man who sentenced a carpenter
to death because he carried the germs of such a
deadly disease? It is that, you know—a most deadly
disease.

(*He pauses and sighs.*)
Why not deny it all? Go home, stop preaching. The
world is what it is, and it will be very much the same
long after you and I are gone.

JOSHUA

You ask me to deny myself.

PILATE

I ask you only to stop being a preacher and agitator.
Be a philosopher. If you believe that men are capable
of love and decency instead of hatred and indecency,
why that is your prerogative. But if you noise it
about, why then you pull the props out of our entire
system. We rule by virtue of greed, hatred, and
indecency. Never forget that, Joshua.

CLAUDIA

I'm hungry.

PILATE

(*to Claudia*)
Yes, my dear.
(*to Joshua*)
Well, Joshua?

JOSHUA

I cannot deny myself.

PILATE

Then you leave me no choice—none at all. We are incompatible, you and me. Either you must die or I must die—and I cherish life, Joshua. Do you?

JOSHUA

(*softly*)
More, I think, than you could ever understand.

PILATE

More's the pity.

Pilate presses a button on his desk, and from his *POV* the door opens and the Centurion comes in, the Romans behind him.

PILATE

(*gesturing at Joshua*)
Take him away.

Joshua stands for a long moment, regarding Pilate. Then he turns and walks to the door, the Romans on either side of him.

89.   INT. THE CORRIDOR IN A PRISON

TRUCKING SHOT as Joshua walks between two Romans, the Centurion leading.

90.   INT. THE CORRIDOR IN A PRISON. ANOTHER ANGLE

As they approach the cell. One of the Romans takes keys out of his pocket and unlocks the cell door. The Centurion motions Joshua in, and then closes the door behind him.
The Centurion locks the door.

91. INT. THE CELL

REVERSE OF 90, as Joshua enters the cell.

This is a large cell, and in it are Frankie, Joey, and Big Abbey. To the left and right as one enters the cell, an upper and lower bed, four beds in all. Across the back of the cell, a bench. At the end of one of the beds, a sink and a toilet.

Frankie lies on his elbow in one of the beds. He has been badly beaten, his face bruised and cut and dry blood on his clothes.

Joey sits at the foot of the same bed. He, too, shows signs of having been beaten.

Big Abbey sits on the bench facing the door of the cell. He still wears a jacket, but is without his tie. He has lost none of his sense of power, his cockiness.

As Joshua enters, the door closing behind him, they all look at him.

JOEY

It's Joshua! Frankie, it's Joshua! Man, we swinging now! I told you he wouldn't let us die here like rats!

BIG ABBEY

(*rising and mockingly*)
The miracle man! Welcome to our cozy little nest.

Joshua looks from face to face. There is only pity on his face when he looks at the two boys.

FRANKIE

(*sitting up*)
Joshua—you a prisoner here, same as us?

JOSHUA

That's right, Frankie—same as you.

FRANKIE

No. No, I don't believe it. Crazy. What for? What
you ever done, Joshua? You never done nothing.
Man, you're pure—

JOSHUA

(*going over to look at Frankie's face*)
Does it hurt, kid?

FRANKIE

Not so much now. It was bad yesterday.

Joshua turns and tilts Joey's face. He touches a cut.
Joey winces.

JOEY

(*desperately*)
Joshua—you got a fix? I'm beginning to shake. I'm
going to blow my stack. I'm going crazy, Joshua. I
got to have a fix.

Joshua shakes his head, and goes to the sink, where he
wets his handkerchief.

JOEY

(*cont'd*)
Joshua, please, man—

BIG ABBEY

Shut up, punk! You blew your stack long ago. Where
in hell's the miracle man going to get a fix? I'm sick
of hearing you whine and whimper.

Joshua squeezes the excess water out of the handkerchief.
Then he goes to the two boys. He cleans Joey's cuts first.

JOSHUA

Easy does it, kid. Easy. Just relax. Don't think about
anything for a little while. Close your eyes. Just
believe that you're warm and safe with good friends
around you. No worry. No trouble. No misery about
any fix—

Grinning, Big Abbey watches as Joshua turns to Frankie
and begins to wipe his face. Frankie winces with pain. Joey
sits with his eyes closed for a moment or two.

FRANKIE

Hurts like a sonovabitch, Joshua.

JOSHUA

I know. Now I'm through. Relax, kid. Just breathe
slowly, easily.

FRANKIE

Sure, Joshua. I'm all right. It's the kid over here. He
never had no brains. Just hooked full of the lousy
stuff and looking for kicks. Always looking for kicks.

Joshua goes back to the sink to wash and squeeze dry his
handkerchief.

BIG ABBEY

Kicks! Lousy little punks!

FRANKIE

God-damn you sonovabitch—what you want us to
do, be beat to death before we tell 'em who give
us the damn gun?

BIG ABBEY

What's the difference, big man? You're crow's meat in the morning anyway. Crow's meat!

JOSHUA

Leave the kids alone, Big Abbey.

BIG ABBEY

(*leaping to his feet and thrusting a finger at Joshua*)
Now listen to me, miracle man. This is my kind of setup here, not yours. And while we're in this crummy, stinking cell, I run things, not you!

JOSHUA

(*shaking his head*)
No.

Big Abbey advances toward Joshua, his hands spread. Joshua watches him, as do the two boys. Then Big Abbey stops.

JOSHUA

(*cont'd softly*)
What kind of a man are you? Doesn't anything reach you? What kind of food is hatred? Look around you. You know where we are.

BIG ABBEY

Talk for yourself, miracle man.

He swings around and goes back to his bench.

JOSHUA

(*to Joey*)
Which is your bed, Joey?
(*Joey nods at the upper, over Frankie.*)
Try to sleep a little, kid.

JOEY

I can't sleep, Joshua. I go crazy when I try to sleep.

JOSHUA

(*sitting down beside him*)
All right, kid. We'll talk.

JOEY

(*almost choking on the words*)
Joshua—man, they going to kill us. You can't just
talk—like it's nothing.

BIG ABBEY

Why didn't you think of that before you plugged
the bank guard, punk?

FRANKIE

Drop dead!

JOEY

(*to Joshua*)
Like it's death, man—death.

JOSHUA

Joey—Joey, do you believe in me?

JOEY

What?

JOSHUA

Do you believe in me, kid?

JOEY

I don't dig you, Joshua. What's to believe? They going to kill us.

Frankie and Big Abbey are listening intently, Frankie hanging on to each word desperately, Big Abbey still with a sneer on his face.

JOSHUA

To believe is to live. Try to understand me, kid.

JOEY

Believe? What's to believe?

JOSHUA

In man and in the son of man—in ourselves, kid, in you and me and Frankie and Big Abbey—

JOEY

(*shaking his head*)
I just don't dig you, Joshua.

JOSHUA

Try, kid—try. Believe in us—like the whole meaning and purpose of the world and the world's existence is

here in this cell with us, and all the things we did,
the bitterness we lived with—all of that is washed
away—

JOEY

(looking at Joshua, his face twisted with pain, his
eyes full of tears)
I'll try, Joshua—

ON THE DOOR now, as it opens, and the Centurion enters.

CENTURION

All of you, on your feet and come with me!

One by one they stand up and file through the door to the
cell, and exit.

92. INT. THE CORRIDOR IN THE PRISON

REVERSE OF 91, as the four prisoners leave the cell and
turn down the corridor at the motion of the Centurion. Three
Romans with submachine guns fall in on either side of the
prisoners, six Romans in all.

CAMERA remains fixed as the prisoners and the Romans
and the Centurion march down the prison corridor, becom-
ing smaller and smaller in the distance.

93. EXT. A STREET IN FRONT OF A BUILDING
WITH BROAD, HIGH STEPS

This is the exterior of the prison. The first necessary quality
are the high steps, so that they may be used as a platform
above the crowd. It would be preferable, but not absolutely
necessary, for the front of the building to be somber.

The street in front of the building is filled with people. They wait quietly, their eyes fixed on the doors to the building, at the top of the steps.

94. EXT. THE STREET. A ROLLS-ROYCE

ESTABLISHMENT on a Rolls-Royce that stands at the edge of the crowd. Claudia and Helen in back. A *CHAUFFEUR* in the driver's seat.

95. INT. THE ROLLS-ROYCE

ON the two women in back, *TWO SHOT* from front.

CLAUDIA

It's so utterly tiresome—wait in the office, wait here —wait for this and wait for that.

HELEN

My dear, it's the price you pay for being number one.

CLAUDIA

Darling, it's the price I'm tired of paying. One of these days, I just won't be waiting.

HELEN

Patience, darling.

CLAUDIA

That's all he says—patience, patience, patience. And these wretched, grubby, impossible people. Just look at them. And that one we saw this morning—like an animal in those filthy clothes he wore—

96.   EXT. ON THE STEPS OF THE PRISON

A mounting drumbeat here as the doors open and the Roman guards emerge with their prisoners.

WIDE AND FULL on the top of the steps.

Pilate stands to one side as guards and prisoners emerge. The Centurion joins Pilate, and reports *sotto.*

Joshua, Frankie, Joey, and Big Abbey are positioned across the top step, facing the crowd. A guard with a tommy gun stands at each side. The four remaining Romans stand behind them.

Now the Centurion steps back from Pilate, as Pilate crosses over, down a single step, and facing the crowd.

Hands on hips, the Centurion watches.

ON PILATE as he observes the crowd, and picking up his POV:

INTERCUT THE CROWD, panning across faces, and then

CLOSE IN on specific faces, Joseph, Mary, Sarah, Salome, Jairus, his wife, Mrs. Marat, storekeeper, customers, and separate from each other, here and there among the crowd, the twelve disciples, and—

CLOSE SPECIFIC on *CARIOT*

and with this, *BIG ABBEY'S HOODLUMS,* the two we have seen in the nightclub and others, a minimum of ten, but so spotted and photographed as to increase their numbers. These hoodlums are flashily dressed, tight tab collars, bright ties, checked coats, bowler hats, hard, tough faces. They should be tall men and placed in juxtaposition to shorter people, so that they stand out.

ABOVE INTERCUTTING during Pilate's speech.

(But before Pilate speaks and from the moment the

doors open for the prisoners to emerge, music specific to the point, a rolling of drums that builds up to crash into silence. Absolute silence as Pilate speaks. *No background music.*)

PILATE

We rule justly, for ours is the power of peace and order, and so the world has peace and order and plenty. Our justice rewards good and punishes evil.
(*He pauses and looks over the crowd.*)

INTERCUT Pilate's *POV.*

PILATE

(*cont'd*)
Yet there are times when we temper justice with mercy. This is such a time. Here are four criminals—
(*He points to the four prisoners.*)
They have done wrong—great wrong. They have plotted and connived and agitated and murdered, and for this they must die.
But we rule many people and many places, and we respect the customs of others and the gods of others. These are your high holy days when you celebrate your feast of the Passover—when it is your custom to give life to a condemned man.
Here are four condemned men. Choose which one you will.

PANNING across the faces of the four men, Joshua, Frankie, Joey, and Big Abbey.

CLOSE on Pilate's face.

CLOSE on Centurion.

Deep silence still.

CLOSE on Cariot, his face drawn, his mouth tight.

CLOSE on Peter:

PETER

Joshua—

CLOSE on Joseph:

JOSEPH

Give me my son.

And now, one after another, the camera picks up the faces of those who love Joshua, the people around him, his family, the disciples:

MARY

Joshua.

ANDREW

Joshua.

SALOME

Joshua.

JAIRUS

Joshua.

MATTHEW

Joshua.

JAMES

Joshua.

MRS. MARAT

Joshua.

SARAH

Joshua.

SIMON

Joshua.

This to the extent that is needed to establish the fact that those who love Joshua do what they may.

CLOSE on Pilate, who is listening, and from him to

FOUR SHOT of the prisoners, and across this a hard shout that carries over the cries for Joshua.

VOICE

Big Abbey!

CLOSE on hoodlum.

HOODLUM

Big Abbey!

CLOSE on 2d hoodlum.

SECOND HOODLUM

Big Abbey!

CLOSE on 3d hoodlum.

THIRD HOODLUM

Big Abbey!

CLOSE on 4th hoodlum.

FOURTH HOODLUM

Big Abbey!

CLOSE AND QUICK on 5th, 6th, 7th, 8th, 9th, and 10th hoodlum, and each time the hard shout: BIG ABBEY!

Now the voices for Joshua are blurred, and as the shouts of the hoodlums increase, they merge into a rhythmical chorus, so that the swelling chant is boomed out:

BIG ABBEY! BIG ABBEY! BIG ABBEY! GIVE US BIG ABBEY! GIVE US BIG ABBEY! GIVE US BIG ABBEY! GIVE US BIG ABBEY!

Now the voices calling for Joshua are drowned out completely, and we hear only the roar for Big Abbey. The faces of the hoodlums, cheeks swollen, mouths wide, flash before us, one after another, back and forth, giving the impression of dozens of his followers in the crowd.

CLOSE on Centurion, as he looks inquiringly at Pilate.

CLOSE on Pilate, as he nods.

CONTINUING chant for Big Abbey.

INTERCUT to CAR INTERIOR, as Helen and Claudia make faces and cover their ears.

FULL SHOT of four men as they listen. Joshua, Frankie, Joey, and Big Abbey.

The Centurion now walks over to Big Abbey and points down to the crowd.

CLOSE on Big Abbey, as he smiles with pleasure and satisfaction.

Then the CAMERA moves back to

WIDE, FULL SHOT as Big Abbey walks down the stairs, his hand raised in greeting.

DEAD SILENCE SUDDENLY for

THREE SHOT on Joshua, Frankie, and Joey.

97. INT. THE SHOP

MORNING, the following day.

Joseph stands grimly at his bench, working slowly, mechanically, planing wood in therapeutic motion, as Mary enters from the apartment in the rear.

MARY

What have you heard?

Her face is drawn, her eyes red with weeping.

JOSEPH

Nothing.
(*He does not turn, goes on working.*)

MARY

But there must be some news.

JOSEPH

I heard nothing. I heard nothing.
(*His voice rises.*)
Why should they tell me? I went to the prison and pleaded, and they looked at me as if I was dirt. Dirt. I said, let me see my son—let me see my son—

Mary goes to him.

MARY

Joseph—Joseph—

For the first time, we see a break in his shell of hardness. He puts down his plane, turns to Mary, and puts his arms around her. Her cheek against his shirt, she continues to sob, her words muffled by his shirt and her emotion.

MARY

Joseph, why should they kill him? What wrong did he ever do? I know you were impatient with him, but all his life, I never heard him say an angry word. Always, he had time to listen to others. Must he die because he showed people how to love— how to find a little peace?

During this, Sarah enters from the apartment, stops to listen to Mary.

CLOSE on her face, and then her POV, as sound of door bursting open.

FULL on door to street as Salome enters, stands panting by the side of the door, one clenched fist thrust into her mouth.

SARAH

What is it, Salome?

SALOME

Oh, my God—my God!

Joseph gently pushes Mary aside and walks toward Salome. He stares at her face. Then he flings the door open, and steps through.

98.   EXT. STREET IN FRONT OF SHOP. JOSEPH'S POV

REVERSE OF 97, as Joseph leaves shop, and then his *POV*:

FULL SHOT ON ANGLE down the street. A confused murmur of mounting noise and shouting, and then we see:

Frankie, Joshua, and Joey walking slowly down the street, not on the sidewalk, but out in the gutter, and each of them staggers under the enormous weight of a cross they bear and drag.

On each side of the three men who bear the crosses, five Romans walk, ten in all and armed with tommy guns. The Centurion leads the way.

Around them, but keeping distance under menace of the tommy guns, a crowd of onlookers, some of them Joshua's followers, some simply curiosity seekers.

(*No music here*)

JOSEPH

(*the cry torn from him*)
My son!

Joseph flings himself toward the procession. A Roman tries to bar his way, but Joseph thrusts him aside, breaks through to Joshua, seizes the cross to lift the burden.

But as he lays hands on the cross, a second Roman whips him across the head with the barrel of the tommy gun. As Joseph staggers, a second and third Roman close in with their billies out, beat Joseph down, and then stand over him, lashing at him with the billies as he lies in the street.

CENTURION

(*loudly*)
Enough of that!

The Roman soldiers fall back into place, and the procession continues.

Mary, Sarah, and Salome rush out to Joseph. Mary falls on her knees next to his recumbent body. Sarah and Salome stand over her—and then look after the crosses. From their POV:

99.   EXT. THE STREET. ANOTHER ANGLE

Looking down toward the end of the street now as the three men walk with their burden.

100.   EXT. ON THE AVENUE

As the three men move down on avenue now. The crowd around them has grown, but their own steps are slower. They weaken and the burden of the crosses grows more terrible.

101.   EXT. ANOTHER PART OF THE AVENUE

FROM ABOVE, rooftop, the crosses being dragged southward, a crowd of people following.

102.   EXT. FURTHER SOUTH
CLOSE on Joshua. His face is tight with fatigue and pain.

CLOSE on Frankie, his cuts open, the blood welling down over his face.

CLOSE on Joey, his face too contorted with pain and fear and fatigue.

PANNING ON THE CROWD.
Various angles for the Romans.

103.   EXT. LOOKING SOUTH, AGAINST MOUNT MORRIS PARK

As the three men emerge from the avenue and drag their crosses across the last street that bounds the park.
The crowd is larger now.

PANNING up the surface of the rock and across as people gather.

LONG SHOTS, down from the rock above, to show people coming from all directions.

104. EXT. THE PATH UP THE ROCK. MOUNT MORRIS

Now, dragging the crosses up the rock, the three men move slowly indeed. They trip and fall, and the Romans kick at them until they rise.

ON JOSHUA as he stumbles and falls under the weight of his cross. The Romans kick him until he rises. Coming behind him, Joey attempts to help him to his feet, while balancing his own burden.
The Centurion runs back.

CENTURION

None of that! I'll have no malingering!

Joshua manages to gain his feet and stagger on.

105. EXT. THE PATH UP MOUNT MORRIS. ANOTHER PART

Closer to the top now.

PANNING across the slopes. People approaching. Kids climbing the walls and cutting across.
The three men with the crosses, the Romans.

CLOSE on the Centurion's face as he leads the procession.

AN ANGLE from below, looking up, the heads of Joshua, Joey, and Frankie visible above a stone wall, the crosses above them.

ANOTHER ANGLE, looking down.

106. EXT. THE PATH UP MOUNT MORRIS

As Joey, Joshua, and Frankie approach the top.
And from the top, as the Centurion steps onto it. His
POV—

PANNING over the top, and then, also from his POV:

The three men, breasting the top with their burdens.

107. EXT. ON TOP OF MOUNT MORRIS

As they reach the top, Frankie collapses to his knees.
Joey stands swaying. Joshua looks around him, and from his
POV:

PANNING across the hazy background of the city, the tall
buildings to the south.
And again from Joshua's POV:

FULL ON the other paths up to the top, as people begin to
appear, not rushing, but coming timidly yet withal driven
by some force they cannot resist—people whose faces we
recognize as familiar from previous passages, and strange faces
as well.

NOW four of the Romans spread out, occupying the four
points of a square about twenty-five feet by twenty-five feet.
They take their places, legs spread, their tommy guns menac-
ing and holding back the crowd.

Joshua, Joey, and Frankie are more or less in the center of
this space. Their strength leaves them, and they collapse on
the ground, allowing their crosses to fall beside them.

INTERCUT the slopes of the park. More and more people,
moving, climbing toward the top.

INTERCUT the park from below, as the people enter and start upward.

CLOSE on the Centurion, and his *POV:*

THREE SHOT of the prisoners. Then the Centurion swings his gaze, and

PANNING over the action on top and then back to the three men. The Centurion approaches them.

CENTURION

(*to the three men*)
Get up.
(*They don't move. His voice hardens.*)
Up, damn you! Get up!

Two Romans advance menacingly, and the three men struggle to their feet.

CENTURION

Take off your clothes!

The three men look at him uncomprehendingly.

CENTURION

(*cont'd*)
I said, take off your clothes!

Now, slowly and painfully, the three men begin to disrobe. Joshua still wears the sheepskin-lined work coat he has worn throughout, and underneath it, his brown shirt, brown pants, and army shoes. Frankie and Joey wear leather jackets.

Piece by piece, they undress, until at last they stand shivering in their underwear shorts. Their clothes lie in an uneven pile.

One of the Romans pulls off Joshua's wristwatch and also a wristwatch Frankie wears, breaking the band in each case. He drops them on the clothes. Another Roman, meanwhile, is going through the pockets of the clothes, removing some change, a good-luck piece from Frankie's pocket, from Joshua's pocket a wallet, keys, a few other things. All this is put in a small pile next to the pile of clothes.

The prisoners stand bent and shivering, Joshua between the two boys.

While this goes on, the other Romans spread out the crosses, so that there will be room for them to work. They seize Frankie first.

FULL on Frankie and two Romans as they drag him to the cross, and then quick

INTERCUT to Joey, in the hands of two other Romans.

CLOSE on Joshua, as he watches this, the pain and horror reflected on his face.

INTERCUT to the crowd for reaction.

FULL on Frankie. He is spread-eagled on the cross, his outstretched hands lashed to it, his feet lashed together above a step support on the bottom.

Then a Roman takes a short, heavy stone hammer and a long railroad spike, sets the spike on Frankie's hand, and drives it home with a brutal blow of the hammer.

FROM FRANKIE:

A WILD CRY OF PAIN

INTERCUT to the crowd.

ON JOEY who is similarly lashed.

BACK ON FRANKIE. There the hammer is raised again, but before it falls,

FROM JOEY:

A WILD CRY OF PAIN

ON JOEY'S FACE, eyes closed, wracked with pain as he lies on the cross on the ground.

ON JOSHUA, CLOSE BUT FULL, and hold on him and against this *hold*, the blows of the hammer, the cries of pain.

Joshua's head is bent slightly. He looks up now, and from his *POV* we see the two crosses raised into position by the Romans, the two boys hanging there.

CLOSE on Joshua.

INTERCUT to crowd.

FULL as the Romans seize Joshua, and then to his *POV*:

AS THE GROUND TILTS DOWN AND SKY FILLS THE SCREEN, the camera the eyes of Joshua as he is flung on his back and lashed to the cross.

HOLD ON THE SKY,

As the blows of the spikes being driven home are heard, and then,

STILL ON SKY, BUT TILTING,

And then, as the cross is raised,

ON THE SKY, TILTING DOWNWARD TO REVEAL TOP OF ROCK, ROMANS BELOW, CROWD BEYOND, THE FACES OF THE CROWD.

TILTING AND SWAYING, GROUND, ROMANS, FACES INTERCUT INTO PATTERN OF PAIN AND CONFUSION AND HORROR.

And then,

OUT OF FOCUS, ALL IN HAZE.

As the haze clears,

BLEND INTO FULL SHOT of Joshua on cross, and then,

BACK CAMERA TO WIDE SHOT of the three crosses, the three men hanging there, blood running from their hands and feet; then

DROPPING FRAME TO GROUND AND FULL of Romans, kneeling over the two piles of clothes and possessions, rolling dice for the division of these miserable spoils. Then to

JOSHUA, FULL AND CLOSE, moving in on him to

CLOSE-UP, and against this, *FRANKIE'S VOICE:*

FRANKIE

Joshua—help me, help me.

And *JOEY'S VOICE:*

JOEY

It hurts, Joshua—help me! It hurts.

STILL ON JOSHUA, CLOSE-UP, as we establish his *POV.* From his *POV:*

HAZE, OUT OF FOCUS,

As he looks at sky and buildings,

OUT OF FOCUS, THEN INTO FOCUS, as his *POV* drops to the crowd, and then,

PANNING OVER CROWD, focusing in upon faces:

Mary, weeping.

Sarah, holding Joshua's mother, weeping.

Salome, her face a stone image of pain.

Peter, wearing his grief.

Cariot, fear and horror.

Big Abbey, hard, calm.

And other faces, faces of people we have met, faces of strangers, faces of pain and grief and horror.

FULL AND WIDE on the three crosses, and then moving to

CLOSE AND THEN CLOSE-UP of Joshua.

His lips part. With great effort, he tries to speak, fails, tries again, and this time the words:

JOSHUA

Father—forgive them—for they know not what they do.

CAMERA BACK AND UP ON CRANE, holding for a moment, and then

UP AND WIDE AS HIGH AS POSSIBLE and then

HELICOPTER SHOT, up from rock, broadening, the rock, the slopes, the whole park with the three crucified men on top, and then up, spreading to the island of Manhattan and finally into the whole spreading haze of the city below.

THE END